ANGRY WITH GOD

Also by Scott R. Frazer

Where Science Meets God

12 Ways Science Reinforces LDS Doctrine

ANGRY WITH GOD

[Understanding the Rules of Earth Life]

SCOTT R. FRAZER

CFI
AN IMPRINT OF CEDAR FORT, INC.
SPRINGVILLE, UTAH

ISBN 13: 978-1-4621-3564-6

Published by CFI, an imprint of Cedar Fort, Inc.
2373 W. 700 S., Springville, UT 84663
Distributed by Cedar Fort, Inc., www.cedarfort.com

Library of Congress Control Number: 2020935367

Cover design by Shawnda T. Craig

Printed in the United States of America

10 9 8 7 6 5 4 3 2 1

Printed on acid-free paper

Contents

Dedication vii

Introduction 1

Chapter 1—Is God to Blame for Tragedy? 5

Chapter 2—Learning Wisdom versus Choosing Righteousness 25

Chapter 3—The Premortal Existence 39

Chapter 4—RULE 1: The Earth Must Be a Place of Faith 49

Chapter 5—RULE 2: You Must Do Work 59

Chapter 6—RULE 3: The Earth Is a Dangerous Place 65

Chapter 7—Learning as a World 77

Chapter 8—RULE 4: You Must Play the Hand You Are Dealt 91

Chapter 9—RULE 5: Temporal Life Must Be Temporary 101

Chapter 10—RULE 6: We Must Suffer the Consequences of Others' Bad Decisions 111

Chapter 11—Everyone Must Obey the Rules of Earth 125

Chapter 12—Prayer: Asking for Exceptions to the Rules 135

Chapter 13—The Problem with Miracles 153

Chapter 14—RULE 7: The Church of Jesus Christ Must Be Staffed with Humans 159

Chapter 15—Our Perceptions of God 167

Epilogue 173

Notes 175

About the Author 184

Dedication

When my daughter Morgan married Chris in the Salt Lake Temple in 2009, she was as happy as a young woman can be in this lifetime. Morgan grew up in The Church of Jesus Christ of Latter-day Saints in Minnesota. Upon graduation from high school, she attended Brigham Young University and greatly enjoyed her years as a student and cheerleader there. With her marriage, she figured that this was the happily ever after phase of her life, as she had always been taught it would be. Then, about a year after the wedding, Chris was diagnosed with melanoma cancer, and his and Morgan's lives radically changed. Chris started on a regime of chemotherapy, with all the pain and nausea that came with it. Morgan and Chris scoured the internet for doctors, treatments, and clinical studies that could offer them the highest probability of success. Chris had surgeries in Seattle and San Francisco, and they moved to San Diego to enroll in a promising clinical trial designed to study the effects of a new cancer-fighting cocktail of drugs.

Chris and Morgan put their lives on hold for two years while Chris endured the misery of chemotherapy treatments. During that time, Morgan called me, often sobbing, to ask me why Heavenly Father was putting Chris and her through such a crisis. What had they done to deserve this? Chris had a cancer that could take him away from her just a year after their marriage. What could they do to repent of their wrongdoings so Chris could be blessed to get better?

I struggled to comfort both Morgan and Chris, but I knew my answers to their questions were weak and unconvincing. Deep down, I knew that

Morgan's questions were based on mistaken perceptions about earth life, God, and prayer. I knew they had not done anything wrong to deserve cancer in their lives. I also knew that this was not Heavenly Father's fault. He did not cause the cancer to strike, and He was as sad about it as any of us. I found numerous quotes by Church leaders that supported my argument. While comforting, these statements did not really explain *how* God was not involved in causing or allowing this crisis to occur.

After the two years of treatments, Chris's doctors and PET scans declared him free of cancer. Paying off the medical bills would continue for years, but my daughter and her husband could return to a more normal young married life. Despite the happy resolution, I could not stop thinking about my incomplete answers to my daughter's questions. This book is a result of years of searching for better answers.

I would like to dedicate this book to all the people who, like my daughter, have ever been angry with God. If you feel that God ignored you during one of the worst trials of your life, this book may help you better understand why God doesn't fix things for you sooner and more often. In your disappointment and despair, you may have been assured by well-meaning friends that it was God's will that you should suffer through this awful time in your life. I want you to know that such counsel is flawed. You need to understand this so you can stop blaming God, even if it's just a little. I hope this book gives you a new perspective of God, the rules He has to obey, and the role He plays in our earthly lives.

INTRODUCTION

IF YOU ARE ANGRY WITH GOD, it is probably for one of two reasons. First, you may be angry at the world that God created. Many of God's children think He could have done a much better job at this task. This world includes natural disasters, cancer, famine, birth disorders, and other real dangers. A sudden and unexpected tragedy may have happened to you or a family member that you have never been able to resolve. Maybe a house fire, an automobile accident, or a natural disaster took away a loved one. One of your children may be having serious medical problems. Doctors have done their best, but they have not been able to resolve the issue. On a broader scale, you may be angry that God allows poverty, wars, racism, and inequality to exist. Why did God build a world that contains such disappointment and despair? Many people simply cannot forgive God for the negative aspects of this world He created.

On the other hand, you may be mad at God because He has not answered an important prayer. You may have needed Him to resolve a personal matter in your life, and He has not done it. Maybe a daughter has lost her way, and God is not helping her find it again. A rebellious child may be addicted to opioids, or your spouse might be unhappy in your marriage. A dear friend may have been fired from his job, or an elderly parent may be just holding on to life. Whatever the case, the situation may look hopeless. You realize that only a miracle from God can rectify the problem, but He is not responding. We know God has the power to make our problem go away, so why doesn't He use it?

I have found that those who are angry with God make up a diverse group indeed. Some of these people attend church services every Sabbath, often feeling guilty about their suppressed anger. Other people who are mad at God have never set foot in a church building. These people are often agnostic and use their anger to confirm their decision to ignore God. Their logic is that if God exists at all, He has created an unfair world and does not deserve their worship. Every time the evening news reports another global tragedy, these disbelievers get the chance to validate their disbelief.

The premise of this book is that anger with God is misplaced, unfair, and based on misunderstandings of the scriptures and the reasons for earth life. God has created a world for us based on a prior eternal pattern. He has established laws on this earth that are required for our learning and instruction. Throughout this book, we will refer to those laws as the Rules of Earth Life. Many people seem to think the rules of earth are God's playthings and that He can dismiss them anytime He wants. This is patently untrue. God Himself must obey the rules of earth, as we will discuss in the following pages.

So God is blamed for many things—personal health issues, divorces, natural disasters, injuries, and death. He is blamed for wars, suppressive governments, and ethnic cleansings. God is blamed for allowing the Crusades of the Middle Ages, the Holocaust of World War II, and other religious atrocities. Earth's history is replete with wars and violence between followers of different religions. Since the perception and worship of God is a main point of contention between such enemies, it is logical, I suppose, to blame God for not stepping in and clearing up the argument. If God stands by and watches crimes against humanity and does not intercede, halt the violence, and punish the oppressors, is He not complicit in the crimes?

Such a question illustrates the misunderstanding of God's unique role in our earth life. He is not simply a powerful sorcerer who can use his magic to stop the evil workings of mankind. Because this needs to remain a world of faith, God cannot even make an appearance and defend Himself. As one might expect, religions around the world defend their God and declare His innocence in causing world tragedies or the mayhem brought about by evil men. But at the same time, some of those religions actively promote the idea that God directs every event that happens in this world, be it good or bad. With that presumption, any natural catastrophe that occurs must be in accordance with God's will. To add insult to injury, religious leaders will then announce that the tragedy was God's will because the people afflicted have sinned and need to repent. Apparently, this is the easiest response to the question of why a tragedy is allowed to kill thousands. Granted, we read in the scriptures of a few cases when famine and war occurred to different people due to their sins. However, in each of these scriptural cases, those afflicted nations had a prophet to tell them why they were being cursed. It does no good for God to afflict a people for sin if they don't know why they are being punished. Such calls to repentance are rare. Of all the droughts and other tragedies the world has seen, only a very few were initiated by God and, as far as we know, they all occurred in the days of the Old Testament.

If you have had a tragedy occur in your life, this book will not offer you condolences or platitudes that are rather common in books about enduring hardship. We will offer evidence that God did not select you or your family for hardship. Such an academic explanation will do little to heal your emotional trauma. Only time, prayer, and love from those around you can do that. So please know that there is a real difference between mentally understanding the reasons for adversity and emotionally dealing with the heartbreak that accompanies it. Having a better mental understanding of the reasons behind tragedy is a needed step in recovery, since many people seem to be unable to take that step. In short, this book endeavors to absolve God of the blame that is so frequently placed on Him during the emotional backlash of our pain and is dedicated to those who have ever been or still are angry with God. If you are outraged and in no mood to read a book that points out the error behind your hostility, then you should probably read no further. If, however, you are curious as to why you might be blaming God unfairly and thus inhibiting your eternal progress, then please read on.

Chapter 1

Is God to Blame for Tragedy?

On August 29, 2005, Hurricane Katrina slammed into New Orleans, Louisiana. The storm caused numerous breaches in the floodwalls and levees around the greater New Orleans area, submerging about 80 percent of the city in over fifteen feet of water. Over a thousand people died, and total property damage was estimated at eighty-one billion dollars. Katrina damaged or destroyed oil-drilling platforms, refineries, businesses, highways, and almost three hundred thousand homes.[1]

Religious leaders, televangelists, politicians, and even Iraq's Al Qaeda announced that Hurricane Katrina had been sent by God to devastate New Orleans because of the decadence and sinfulness there. After all, New Orleans was the home of Mardi Gras, the French Quarter, and had a well-publicized history of decadence. To some, it seemed an ideal target for God's punishment. These pronouncements became a hot topic of debate and received much media attention. However, in the October general conference of that year, President Gordon B. Hinckley of The Church of Jesus Christ of Latter-day Saints strongly rebutted the accusation. Speaking of Hurricane Katrina, he stated, "Now, I do not say, and I repeat emphatically that I do not say or infer, that what has happened is the punishment of the Lord. Many good people, including some of our faithful Latter-day Saints, are among those who have suffered."[2]

The question of whether God is to blame for tragedy and disaster has been asked for thousands of years. The book of Job in the Old Testament, which debates this one question for forty chapters, is actually one of the oldest books in the Bible, having been written around 587 BC. In this ancient document, Job and his friends each expressed their own opinions as to whether disaster is God's punishment for sin and whether blessings are His reward for obedience. Apparently, a large number of people are still pondering that religious puzzle.

In 1981, Rabbi Harold S. Kushner wrote the book *When Bad things Happen to Good People*,[3] and it became a national best seller. You will still find a number of books with similar titles available for purchase.[4] So, after twenty-five hundred years of debate, faithful believers in God are still seeking for reasons for the tragedies in their lives. A few months ago, a young man sitting next to me on an airplane asked me what God was trying to teach him through the heartbreak of his recent divorce. A good friend in church confessed that he felt that his job loss could well have been divine retribution for the mistakes and follies of his life. The question remains for many people: Does God punish His wayward children by sending misfortune into their lives and not answering their prayers?

Despite the evidence, many people still believe that God sends punishments to individuals who do not meet His expectations. Many faithful Christians seem especially willing to believe that God is punishing *them* personally whenever tragedy strikes someone they love. There are a number of reasons for this belief. Some are scriptural, most of which we find in the Old Testament, but we often blame God for the bad things that happen to us simply because He appears to be the most logical choice.

Tragedies are both overwhelming and life changing. When tragedy occurs, you immediately realize that, from that moment on, your life will never be the same. A disabling health condition, a traumatic divorce, or the death of a loved one can have such a devastating effect on our lives that it is nearly impossible to believe it could be a random event. Thus, we think that if we can just discover God's reasoning behind the tragedy then we might be able to do something to fix it. At the very least, if we could just come to understand *why* the disaster occurred, it would make us feel better. Was this a punishment? Did I do something wrong to cause this, or could I have prevented it? Was it all part of some greater plan? The uncertainties can consume us, so we turn to God, asking in prayer why each misfortune occurs, even while suspecting that this heartbreak was initiated or at least sanctioned by Him. Who else is better to blame? Obviously, God has the power to initiate a crisis that will cause us grief for the rest of our lives. For many tragedies, such as a fast-acting cancer, a heart attack, a devastating hurricane, or the birth of a handicapped baby, it seems that God is actually the *only* one we can logically blame. Some Christians debate that there is a big difference in whether Heavenly Father actually initiated the crises or simply stood back and allowed it to occur. In the midst of heartbreak, the difference between the two possibilities appears minimal. In the end, many hold God responsible for their grief.

Stages of Grief

Everyone has probably been mad at God at some point in his or her life. It appears to be a natural reaction to tragedy. The grieving process has been broken down into five stages: denial, anger, bargaining, depression, and acceptance.[4] God has a central role in *two* of these stages. After getting past the first stage of denying that the tribulation even occurred, we move on to anger. We may be angry with ourselves for not somehow preventing the problem, but in many cases, we realize that we simply did not have the power to prevent the adversity. Then we realize that God *did* have the power to avert the tragedy, and our anger swings toward Him for not *using* His power. As stated in the book *On Grief and Grieving*:

> The truth is that anger has no limits. It can extend not only to your friends, the doctors, your family, yourself, and your loved one who died, but also to God. You may ask, "Where is God in this? Where is his love? His powerfulness? His compassion? Is this really God's will?" There you sit, alone with your anger, wondering how to reconcile your spirituality and your religion with this loss and anger.[5]

After the anger, we then usually enter the bargaining stage of grief. God plays a major role in this stage as well, because He is usually the one we are trying to sell on the possibility of a new outcome. From the same book quoted above:

> Before a loss, it seems you will do anything if only your loved one may be spared. "Please, God," you bargain, "I will never be angry at my wife again if you'll just let her live." After a loss, bargaining may take the form of a temporary truce. What if I devote the rest of my life to helping others? Then can I wake up and realize this has all been a bad dream?[6]

When the bargaining does not work, we get angry with God yet again. We then enter into the depression stage of our grieving. While there are grief counselors and bereavement groups available for support, personal adversity often plunges once-faithful Christians into a dark place from which they never emerge. This is when many disaffected believers decide that God does not exist or, if He does, He does not deserve their faith and obedience. Even after they move on with their secular lives, these new agnostics may never regain their spiritual lives. When a man blames God for a hardship, he often carries that anger with him for the rest of his life, until he can finally, as the saying goes, "curse God and die."

Blaming God

Blaming God for disaster is endemic in our society. Somehow, the popular conclusion in religious circles has been that, since God is all-powerful, absolutely everything that happens in the world is His will. This is a terrible accusation to lay on our loving Heavenly Father, but we see it every day. When a young man dies in the prime of his life, the sympathies often expressed to the grieving parents are, "God called him home" or "God has another mission for him in Heaven" or "It is all in God's plan." This implies that God arranged the death of this young man to get him from the mortal world to the afterlife a little more quickly. It infers that this young man apparently had talents that God could not find elsewhere in heaven, so He arranged for the death of their son. What a terrible concept to suggest to grieving parents! In such sympathies, mourners essentially express their opinion that, "Yes, God did take the life of your son, but I am sure it was for a very good reason." If they actually believed that God had taken their son, could his loving parents ever forgive Him? To all parents who have lost a child, let me assure you that it was never God's will that such a thing should happen. God joins you in your grief. He did not cause it.

But the idea that we should blame God for our difficulties extends even further. I have heard numerous Church members describe a painful physical ailment, a distressing family problem, or a serious financial setback and then exclaim that they have fasted and prayed to understand *what God was trying to teach them* through this awful event! The implication here is that God initiated a devastating loss of their happiness to get them to guess what they were doing wrong and correct it. By this faulty logic, it would appear that God will arrange for cancer to afflict an elderly grandmother in order to further humble her, teach her pain, or cause her to repent of some unknown sin. Where did this belief come from? Religions have taught for many years that God influences even the smallest details of our lives. On one hand, it may be a comforting thought that God interacts with us so closely in each moment of our lives. Such a belief assures us of God's love and our importance.

On the other hand, if we believe that God influences our lives daily, then God is on the hook for many disappointments. Did you get the flu because your body is susceptible to a virus or because God gave it to you? Did your car break down because you drove it so much or because God thought you needed another financial setback? Were you late for work because you left home too late or because God delayed traffic to teach you responsibility? Then, if we accept the premise that God causes the small, day-to-day difficulties in our lives, isn't it a forgone conclusion that He is the author of the major tragedies as well? This belief has caused many afflicted people to feel so much undeserved guilt that they consciously choose to become atheists. If God causes the calamities in our lives, they conclude, He must have a very sadistic side and does not merit their worship.

You may logically argue that God sends us difficulties and disaster to make us *better people*. By this line of thinking, God decides which tribulations are necessary in our lives to help us mature, develop empathy, and handle grief. Once He has made the decision, God then uses His power to bring the needed hardship into our lives. This concept is based on the fact that difficulties really *do* help us mature, develop empathy, and handle grief. The truth of that principle has been proven in millions of life stories. We have a lot of learning to acquire from childhood to adulthood, but maturity is caused by life experiences, not age. Afflictions teach us perseverance, strength, empathy, patience, and appreciation of our normal day-to-day lives. Any negative mishap in our lives gives us the opportunity to respond and further develop our courage and resilience—or to retreat and ignore the difficulty. Life experiences motivate us to grow, and I am thankful to live in a world that provides them. But there are problems with the conclusion that God custom designs our tragedies and springs them upon us. First, it has very little scriptural basis, which we will examine in a moment. Second, one has to wonder if the thousands of people affected by a hurricane, earthquake, or other natural disaster were all due for both a near-fatal experience and a lesson in humility by losing their homes.

For example, in November 2018, the camp fire in Paradise, California, destroyed 13,053 homes.[7] Did the families in those homes all need this particular hardship in their lives? Certainly not. It would have been an incredible coincidence indeed if almost all of the population in Paradise needed such a severe lesson in humility and appreciation. Will each of those 13,053 families learn to be more resilient and thankful as they build new homes and lives? Almost certainly. So, while we know that disaster strengthens character, it is illogical to extrapolate that God sends those disasters.

When a ship at sea sinks, drowning everyone on board, it is impossible to ascribe the disaster to God trying to teach those passengers a lesson. Last, if God strikes me with tragedy to improve *my* obedience, is His plan also to cause my wife, children, grandchildren, friends, and neighbors new emotional pain to develop their empathy as well? Do they also deserve punishment, or are they simply collateral damage to the disaster sent to me? No, the long-held belief that God sends misfortune into our lives to teach us principles is rife with impossibilities, gaps in logic, and lack of proof. Joseph Smith stated,

> So that it is an unhallowed principle to say that such and such have transgressed because they have been preyed upon by disease or death, for all flesh is subject to death."[8]

However, that "unhallowed principle" seems to be the exact premise of the Book of Job, which is why we will now examine this scripture and our conclusions about it.

The Book of Job

The book of Job is the classic go-to scripture when it comes to defending the idea that bad things are sent by God to afflict us. Job and his friends Eliphaz, Bildad, Zophar, Elihu, and the Lord debate the topic for thirty-nine chapters. The saying "curse God and die" actually comes straight out of the book of Job. After Job has lost all of his children and wealth and is covered with boils from head to foot, Job's wife exclaims, "Dost thou still retain thine integrity? curse God and die" (Job 2:9). Job then answers her with a statement that deserves admiration yet seems to support the idea that disaster and tragic loss come from God. "What? Shall we receive good at the hand of God, and shall we not receive evil?" (Job 2:10). Several other verses from Job support the idea that God chastens us with tragedy. These verses are all statements made by Job or his friends in defense of God or to indicate an acceptance of fate.

> Naked came I out of my mother's womb, and naked shall I return thither: the LORD gave, and the LORD hath taken away; blessed be the name of the LORD. (Job 1:21)

> Behold, happy is the man whom God correcteth: therefore despise not thou the chastening of the Almighty: For he maketh sore, and bindeth up: he woundeth, and his hands make whole. (Job 5:17–18)

It should be noted again that the book of Job is an ancient book, written at the time of Israel's exile to Babylon in the fifth century. Job is chronologically misplaced in the latter half of the Old Testament, as it now appears to be one of the oldest books in the Bible. Thus, the question, "Does God bless the righteous and curse the sinners?" has been asked for millennia. Until recently, it was believed Job's answer to this question was an unqualified "yes," but our understanding has now changed.

The Impatience of Job

Ironically, while Job has been quoted liberally to argue that God rewards the righteous and punishes wrongdoers, it actually teaches the exact opposite. In his excellent book "Rereading Job," Michael Austin details the needed adjustments to our thinking regarding Job. First, Austin announces that the book of Job was *not* a historical rendition of a real man named Job.

> Job is a highly stylized work of imaginative literature that may or may not have been based on the experience of a real person but cannot be considered objective history. Everything about the Book of Job announces that it is a work of literature. It begins with the Hebrew equivalent of "once upon a time" and deliberately steers us away from any historical place or period. It features immortal characters (God and Satan) acting in ways that are inconsistent with their actions anywhere else in the Bible.[9]

Since my youth, I never liked the book of Job, since I could never reconcile the premise that God put Job through hell on earth just to win a petty argument with Satan. If Job is a historically accurate book, then no matter how one tries to justify the narrative, it is rather difficult to see God in a favorable light. So, it was a huge relief for me to learn that the book of Job is actually a work of literature and not historical fact. If Job is not historical, then God did not really make a bet with Satan to see how far Job could be pushed. He did not allow Job's ten children to be killed or Job to be stricken with disease as part of that wager. If the book of Job is a work of literature, then God did not really bully and intimidate the man Job in chapters 38–41.

Austin presents good arguments that Job is not historical. Many Church members believe that Job must be a real person, because the argument is made that he is referred to by Ezekiel in Ezekiel 14:14, by James in James 5:11, and by the Savior in Doctrine and Covenants (D&C) 121:10. However, the Savior also refers to the beggar Lazarus in Luke 16:19–31, the Good Samaritan in Luke 10:33, and the prodigal son in Luke 15:11, never mentioning that these men *were not real.* Fictional characters are often used to teach, as demonstrated in Aesop's fables, Grimm's fairy tales, stories by Hans Christian Anderson, the Tales of Arabian nights, and Jesus's parables. The story of Job does not have to be historical to instruct us about earth life and how we should behave.

If Job is not historical, then what is the point of Job? Good literature is supposed to not only entertain the reader but also teach a concept as well. Job is good literature, but since the book uses irony to teach its lesson, many readers have missed its point. Actually not having to justify the book of Job as historical frees the reader to seriously evaluate the message behind the story. Rereading Job in that light reveals a rather shocking reversal of perspective.

Austin goes on with his explanation of the complexity of the book of Job.

> The Book of Job contains two basic parts: a simplistic prose frame and a complicated long poem, with the latter designed to comment ironically on the former. The Job frame, which consists of chapters 1–2 and 42:7–16, tells the tale of a righteous man who suffers extreme misfortune, endures them all with patience and faith, and gets rewarded handsomely in the end for being such a good sport.[10]

This "frame" is the story of Job that most of us remember. This is the story of how God allowed Satan to afflict a righteous man with all manner of financial ruin, family death, and disease. Yet Job suffers valiantly, defends God, and is blessed tenfold in the end. In further evidence of the irony of the frame, Job fathers exactly seven sons and three daughters to replace the seven sons and three daughters who died at the beginning of the story. But valiant suffering for no cause is NOT the lesson taught in chapters 3–41 of the same book. In the poem portion of the book, Job attacks the conventional wisdom that God blesses the righteous and punishes the wicked. At times Job's argument with his friends gets quite heated, but Job flatly refuses to confess the sins his friends suggest he committed. Thus, chapters 3–41 of Job are a complete reversal of the principle that most Christians take away from reading the book of Job. Job is not patient. Job does not accept his fate without complaint. When his friends state that Job has sinned to bring tragedy upon his own head, Job boldly defends himself.

> I put on righteousness, and it clothed me: my judgment was as a robe and a diadem. I was eyes to the blind, and feet was I to the lame. I was a father to the poor: and the cause which I knew not I searched out. And I brake the jaws of the wicked, and plucked the spoil out of his teeth. (Job 29:14–17)

Eliphaz, Bildad, and Zophar continue to defend the age-old belief that God punishes the wicked and blesses the righteous, so they reason that Job must have sinned. Job, however, does not relent. He challenges the Almighty or any adversary to provide a list of his crimes (Job 31:35). Setting up a storybook frame and then a poem that mocks the tale is a complicated piece of literature. The author of the book of Job subtly makes his statement that tragedy cannot be used as a discerner of righteousness, as was commonly believed at the time. Those who obey God are often struck down with awful calamity, frequently for simply being in the wrong place at the wrong time.

It is enlightening to reread Job with the new understanding that it actually attacks the premise that God afflicts each of us individually, whether we are righteous or wicked. This learning also means that we can also no longer in good conscience use the book of Job to argue that God sends adversity into your life for no apparent reason. Unfortunately, while the book of Job repeatedly *asks* why bad things happen to good people, it never really *answers* the question.

Punishments of Individuals in the Scriptures Are Rare

Many good Christians, who don't want to blame God for fatal catastrophes, take a compromise belief that God may not cause natural disasters, but He will put mishaps and stumbling blocks along our individual life's path. But this belief has little to no scriptural basis. The Lord does, of course, foretell the punishments that will befall a wayward people.

> I will also send wild beasts among you, which shall rob you of your children, and destroy your cattle, and make you few in number; and your high ways shall be desolate. (Leviticus 26:22)

> For, behold, the Lord cometh out of his place to punish the inhabitants of the earth for their iniquity: the earth also shall disclose her blood, and shall no more cover her slain. (Isaiah 26:21)

> Therefore thus saith the Lord of hosts, Behold, I will punish them: the

> young men shall die by the sword; their sons and their daughters shall die by famine. (Jeremiah 11:22)

These Old Testament verses threaten to punish a particular *nation*—be it Israel, Judah, or one of their enemies. These peoples were sinning, and there would be consequences to their bad decisions. However, there are a few times in the scriptures that the Lord punishes an *individual* to get him to change his ways. Sometimes the Lord promises to punish a king, but generally the king actually represents his entire people.

In my review of the Old Testament, I find individual punishments of Cain (Genesis 4:11–12), the false prophet Shemaiah (Jeremiah 29:32), a servant of Elisha (2 Kings 5:27), and King Uzziah (2 Chronicles 26:19). In a quick review of the New Testament, only Herod (Acts 12: 23), Elymas (Acts 13:11), and Ananias and Sapphira (Acts 5:5, 10) are punished as individuals. Even then, three of these four people *died* as a result of their punishment, so it is unlikely that God was trying to teach them something or even bring them to repentance. Paul had a vision and then three days of blindness and fasting, but that was more to gain his attention and aid in the conversion process than to get him to repent.

Similarly, the Book of Mormon has only a few individuals who receive direct-from-the-Lord punishments. *As a people*, the Nephites were cursed numerous times with famine or war to get them to repent. But there was never a time when an individual was punished to get him to repent of a wrongdoing. Korihor demanded to see a sign from God and was struck dumb (Alma 30:49–50), which led to his death soon after. Sherem *also* demanded a sign from Jacob and he was given one, which led to his death as well (Jacob 7:14–15). (From these two examples, it appears that asking for a sign is *never* a good idea, so I don't recommend it.) Other bad guys in the Book of Mormon were not punished by God. Nehor preached false doctrine to the Nephites in the first chapter of Alma. When Gideon, a righteous man and hero of the people, publicly disagreed with his teachings, Nehor attacked and killed him. For this murder, Alma had Nehor executed (Alma 1: 15). The Lord did not punish Nehor. This was simply an instance of capital punishment by the Nephite government.

King Noah was also an unrighteous leader of the Nephite people. When the Lamanites attacked his people, Noah commanded that his personal guard abandon their wives and children and flee with him (Mosiah 19:11). Later, when those men repented of their abandonment and wanted to return to their families, Noah forbade it. For that command, the king's men put Noah to death by fire. Again, this was not the Lord's decision or execution. King Noah's cowardice and poor leadership caused his own men to rebel and kill him. Evil men may enjoy brief success, but eventually their unrighteous decisions bring mortal consequences. Alma the Younger had an experience very similar to Paul's (Mosiah 27:23). Granted, Alma had a tough couple of days of repentance, but his temporary coma could hardly be called a tragedy sent to afflict him.

So throughout the scriptures, we find very few *individuals* who were punished directly by God to motivate them to repent. Many people die in consequence of their choices, such as choosing to fight in a war against their nation's enemies. Whole cities were struck down for their wickedness, such as Sodom & Gomorrah in the Old Testament (Genesis 19:24) and Jacobugath, Laman, Josh, Gad, and Kishkumen in the Book of Mormon (3 Nephi 9:9–10). But there is no scriptural basis to believe that God regularly spotlights individuals for their sins and sends down punishments. It is a rare occurrence. If you think that God is punishing you individually for your misdeeds, you are either in a select group of people or you are blaming God for punishments He did not inflict.

You will hear numerous anecdotal stories from faithful members who believe that God punishes individuals to get them to change their ways. "God sent me pneumonia so I would appreciate good health and attend the temple more often." "God let my son be in a near-fatal auto accident to get him to come back to church." "God allowed me to get cancer so my children would visit and appreciate me more." These conclusions are based on poor reasoning. It is well known that the human mind tends to seek (and thus find) cause and effect in our life experiences. Thus, when a tragedy occurs in our life, we look for a cause. "What did I do to deserve this?" is so common it has become a cliché. A serious tribulation, we believe, is too meaningful and life changing to be random. When we can't identify an immediate cause, we wait. When something good occurs to us a short time later (as it must), we attempt to devise how our misfortune somehow precipitated events that led to a fortunate outcome. In order to explain the two events, we extrapolate a cause-and-effect relationship between them, despite the fact that we have no evidence for such a conclusion. As explained by Marvin J. Ashton,

> We must remember that all suffering is not punishment. It is imperative that we do not allow ourselves to be destroyed by the conduct of others.

> Sometimes we spend so much time trying to determine what we did wrong in the past to deserve the unpleasant happenings of the moment that we fail to resolve the challenges of the present . . . It is important that we not look upon our afflictions as a punishment from God. True, our actions may cause some of our problems, but often there is no evident misconduct that has caused our trials. Just the normal journey through life teaches us that nothing worthwhile comes easy.[11]

The belief that God spends His time planning disasters and tribulations for us goes against all belief that He is a loving Heavenly Father.

One last scripture needs to be highlighted to demonstrate that God does not individually curse the wicked and bless the righteous. As He was explaining the differences between the Mosaic law and His updated law, the Savior said,

> But I say unto you, Love your enemies, bless them that curse you, do good to them that hate you, and pray for them which despitefully use you, and persecute you; That ye may be the children of your Father which is in heaven: for he maketh his sun to rise on the evil and on the good, and sendeth rain on the just and on the unjust. (Matthew 5:44–45)

With this teaching, the Savior puts to rest any remnant of the Old Testament idea that God sends curses upon the wicked. Like Nehor and King Noah, the wicked will suffer consequences for their evil actions, but our Heavenly Father is not the source of those consequences. Instead, He still loves His wicked children and sends sunshine and rainfall upon them and their crops. As Matthew states just a couple of verses later, loving your enemies is a step toward becoming perfect, even as our Father in Heaven is perfect. The sooner we can accept the fact that God is not the source of our misfortunes, the sooner we can stop blaming Him for them.

Then Why Doesn't God Answer My Prayers?

Throughout the New Testament and Book of Mormon, the Savior and other Church leaders encourage us to pray. For most Christians, this instruction remains current today, and we pray as a people. However, during the Enlightenment of the eighteenth century, many people and even Church leaders began to question the power of prayer—and its answers. As explained by one historian:

> The concept of *revelation* was of central importance to traditional Christian theology. The Enlightenment witnessed the development of an increasingly

> critical attitude to the very idea of supernatural revelation . . . The new emphasis upon the mechanical regularity and orderliness of the universe . . . raised doubts about the New Testament accounts of *miraculous happenings*.[12]

Over the years, many Christians and their churches have come to doubt or deny the possibility of revelation and miracles. As a result, today we have a broad range of expectations of God during prayer. Many people still have extreme faith in the power of prayer and in the miraculous blessings of a loving Heavenly Father. Other Christians have few expectations of God, wishing only to express thanks to Him for blessings received. Wherever you are on this spectrum, you must realize that answers to prayers, like God's miracles, must meet certain criteria.

As a child, I was taught that our Heavenly Father is a white-bearded old man whose sole purpose was to answer my prayers and give me blessings. As I grew older and my prayers grew more complex, I realized that God was not a "benevolent grandfather" who gives us things and removes hardships. I changed my thinking due to a number of difficult circumstances that occurred during a disastrous professional career. Though my wife and I prayed mightily about every job offer, we never got sure answers. Each job turned out to be a difficult work environment, a harsh boss, or the continued threat of layoffs. I could have blamed God for not providing better guidance, but I realized the decisions were mine and I paid the consequences for those decisions.

In discussing the harsh rules of earth and consequences of poor (though well-intentioned) decisions, transitions in our thinking must often occur. Our understanding of God should include the fact that He is the Ruler over our mortal probation. He is still our Heavenly Father, but He also assures that our lives on earth meet the requirements of all such earths. In my discussions, I have found that many who are angry with God are actually mad at their benevolent grandfather image of Him. A grandfather will always be kind, protect us, and fix our problems, so giving up that image may be difficult. But neither our Heavenly Father nor Jesus Christ is our frail, sweet grandfather. Their roles are much more complex than that. An understanding of that difference is especially important when we pray, as illustrated in the following example.

When we pray for God to intercede in our lives and fix something, we are offering an "intercessory prayer." The most well known intercessory prayer in history was offered by our Savior in the Garden of Gethsemane. There, in anguish about the painful Atonement that He was about to experience, the Savior prayed, "O my Father, if it be possible, let this cup pass from me" (Matthew 26:39). So, on the eve of the first Good Friday, God the Father had two choices. On one hand, His only begotten son Jesus Christ had just requested that He *not* have to pass through the Atonement. On the other hand, for the plan of salvation to continue, Jesus *had* to pass through the Atonement. Heavenly Father knew that a Savior absolutely had to be provided for all mankind—and this was obviously the greater need. As we all know, the request of the most famous intercessory prayer ever offered was *not* granted. The Savior had to drink from the bitter cup and suffer the pains of the Atonement.

Millions of intercessory prayers are offered up to God every hour of every day. God loves us, and I believe He sincerely wants to grant every one of those requests, but He is bound by His commitment to the plan of salvation. Even when His only begotten Son pled for a way around that plan, our Heavenly Father did not allow it.

The Higher Law

Parents have a unique perspective on understanding higher laws, so perhaps an example from raising children is in order. Do you remember watching your toddler son learn to walk? I do. I remember watching him take a step away from the support of our couch to make his way across the family room. I remember seeing him tilt precariously, overcorrect, and then crash down on his diapered bottom. I also remember as he looked up at me and gave me a pouty look that said in no uncertain terms, "Why did you let *that* happen?"

In the eyes of my young son, I (his earthly father) *was* all-loving, all-knowing, and all-powerful. I dearly loved my son, but I also realized that learning to walk was a requirement of earth life. I saw the misstep, the overcorrection, and that the fall was going to occur. If I had been hovering over him (as I had done for several weeks), I would have had the power to prevent the fall, but I didn't do that this time. There was a higher purpose in allowing the fall to occur—my son needed to learn to walk on his own. Once he had suffered enough consequences of the misstep/overcorrection combination, my son learned to adjust his stride, thus achieving the delicate balance required to walk. There were more falls as my son learned to navigate school, drive a car, hold a job, be happily married, and raise a family. I saw some of his missteps, but had no choice other than to allow many of them to occur.

Sometimes consequences really are the best teachers. Identifying and obeying higher laws is not easy, but it is the better choice. My son is now a good man with a beautiful wife and children. I am proud of my son—and he walks just fine, thank you.

If the Rules of Earth Are Disobeyed, Can God Cease to Be God?

Another scripture explains the concept that God must protect the rules of earth. It is found in chapter 42 of Alma in the Book of Mormon. I believe this is one of the more underappreciated but significant doctrines revealed in the latter days.

> Therefore, according to justice, the plan of redemption could not be brought about, only on conditions of repentance of men in this probationary state, yea, this preparatory state; for except it were for these conditions, mercy could not take effect except it should destroy the work of justice. Now the work of justice could not be destroyed; if so, *God would cease to be God.* (Alma 42:13; italics added)

What? God could actually cease to be God? How can that be, and *how* would it work? Would God be fired by some higher power? Would a new God be sent to take His place? This verse is not a misprint. The phrase "cease to be God" is repeated in Alma 42:22, Alma 42:25, and Mormon 9:19. I believe this is a unique doctrine of Latter-day Saints; no other Christian religion teaches that God could ever cease to be God.

From these and other verses in Alma, it seems that there are eternal, strictly upheld laws governing the balance of justice and mercy. Justice must be satisfied and cannot be cheated by mercy. Mercy can only claim those who have sufficiently repented of their sins. Obviously, the plan of redemption must follow these eternal laws. Actions demand consequences, and mercy can interfere with that process only in rare circumstances. It appears that one of God's most important responsibilities is to ensure that His plan remains in accordance with that law. Amazingly, if He doesn't do His job, then it's apparently possible for Him to *lose* that job. I don't know how God could cease to be God, but I also don't think it will ever happen. God knows the plan of redemption must be allowed to proceed according to plan, and He has maintained that plan for millennia. God will not allow the plan of salvation to be undermined now.

To better appreciate this point, we must consider how important earth life is in the plan of redemption. Earth life is the stage in our eternal progress in which we live, meet with challenges and temptations, and make decisions. We will decide to be good or not, and to repent or not. We will then be judged by justice and mercy on those decisions. Earth life is hard—and it was meant to be. If God puts us on the earth to be tested but then bails us out of every challenge because we ask Him to do so, is it a real test? As will be discussed later, we can and should approach God in prayer to reduce the number and severity of the challenges in our lives. We must realize that God cannot be so merciful that we learn nothing in our mortal probation. We are here to learn from the earth, and He cannot short circuit that process. God is bound to carry out His responsibility. To do less is not in His nature.

The world was designed to teach us principles that could not be taught in the premortal existence. Our Heavenly Father, Jesus Christ, and others put a lot of time and effort into creating this earth, filling it with life and arranging for us to be born here in our appointed time and place. We are here for good reasons. We must experience and learn many things. It is God's responsibility to maintain the environment that will allow our education and testing to continue. As George Q. Cannon explained,

> There is one thing certain, every Latter-day Saint who is faithful to the truth and who lives to the ordinary age of man will have all the opportunities of this kind he or she can desire to gain experience and to have his or her zeal, integrity, courage and devotion to the truth fully exhibited.[13]

As Apostle Jeffrey R. Holland put it:

> God wants us to be stronger than we are—more fixed in our purpose, more certain of our commitments, eventually needing less coddling from him, showing more willingness to shoulder some of the burden of his heavy load. In short, he wants us to be more like him.[14]

God Is Not All-Powerful

Many of those who are angry with God have arrived at their anger due to the belief, taught to them since childhood, that God the Father is all-loving, all-knowing, and all-powerful. But this teaching does not stand up under a simple examination, which critics have used repeatedly to attack God and religion. Looking at the definition of the wording, if our Heavenly Father was all-loving, He would want His children to be joyful and to avoid distress. Yes, He wants us to learn life's lessons, but you would expect Him to spare us as much pain as possible and certainly prevent us from an early death as we learn those lessons. If He was all-knowing, God would know what events were going to lead to our sorrow or death. Finally, if He was all-powerful, God would easily to be able to divert all that misfortune from our lives to keep us constantly happy, content, and alive. But in the real world, tragedy occurs every day. Young people die every day, so, critics conclude, God cannot be all-loving, all-knowing, and all-powerful at the same time. Their logic is undeniable and one has to examine this childhood belief for its flaws.

I believe that God is all-knowing and all-loving, but by definition, God is not all-powerful. Our Heavenly Father is not like the Greek god Zeus, who never practiced any self-governance at all. In fact, our God must follow numerous rules. God cannot lie (Titus 1:2, D&C 62:6). He cannot allow mercy to rob justice (Alma 42:25). God must maintain the earth as a place of faith, severely limiting the options He has for answering prayers. When faced with a prayer request, God must always opt for the "higher law." Simply put, God established commandments for His children on earth, but the plan depends on *His* obedience to the rules He has set for Himself.

Letting go of the perception that God is all-powerful also relieves Him of the indictment that He allowed the Holocaust, ethnic cleansings, and other great massacres of Earth's history. Understanding that God does not have veto power over man's oppressions of their fellow man casts Him in a completely different light. No longer is God the divine being who causes your tribulation and then comforts you through it. Knowing that God has power but *can't* help you is very different from thinking that God has power and simply *won't* help you. As Rabbi Harold S. Kushner explains in *When Bad Things Happen to Good People*,

> If we have grown up, as Job and his friends did, believing in an all-wise, all-powerful, all-knowing God, it will be hard for us, as it was hard for them, to change our way of thinking about Him . . . But if we can bring ourselves to acknowledge that there are some things that God does not control, many good things become possible. We will be able to turn to God for things He can do to help us, instead of holding on to unrealistic expectations of Him which will never come about. We can be angry at what has happened to us, without feeling that we are angry at God.[15]

The line of reasoning that God specially prepares the tragedies in our lives is a frightening misunderstanding of our Heavenly Father, Jesus Christ, and earth life. This book is dedicated to arguing against such an indictment.

Could a loving Heavenly Father devise hardships and tragedies for each of His children on a daily basis? What an awful job that would be! Who would ever aspire to be a god who has the duty and responsibility to continuously afflict His own children? God did create this world, knowing that it would provide us all the challenges and dangers we need to experience in order to learn wisdom while here. You may want to blame God for the earth's design, but scriptures indicate that ours is the same blueprint that has been followed in the creations of other planets for millions of years (Moses 1: 37–39).

In any case, God is on our side in this struggle. He is not a double agent, comforting and encouraging us one moment and then devising our misfortunes the next. The Savior recognized that each day on earth would bring us challenges, evil men, and misfortune. So daunting are these challenges that our Savior encourages us to deal with them one day at a time.

> Take therefore no thought for the morrow: for the morrow shall take thought for the things of itself. Sufficient unto the day is the evil thereof. (Matthew 6:34)

Thus, God does not have to custom design new challenges for us each morning. Earth, and the evil men on it, provide all the dangers, sicknesses, wars, hunger, and difficulties that we will ever need to prove ourselves and help us learn. Since God created the earth, one could still blame Him for the difficulties it provides, but the earth was designed for a purpose, which will soon be discussed. Dangers and difficulties had to be a part of the program.

The Rules of Earth Are Shared by Other Worlds

In Moses 1:33, the Lord tells Moses "And worlds without number have I created; and I also created them for mine own purpose; and by the Son I created them." This revelation must have been intriguing to Moses, but the Lord refused to divulge any details about these other worlds.

> But only an account of this earth, and the inhabitants thereof, give I unto you. For behold there are many worlds that have passed away by the word of my power. And there are many that now stand, and innumerable are they unto man; but all things are numbered unto me, for they are mine and I know them. (Moses 1:35)

So all we really learn from these verses is that there are other planets besides earth, and these planets had or now have inhabitants. We believe those inhabitants are also sons and daughters of our Heavenly Father. They too are living their lives on their planet, proving themselves. They too will pass through a final judgment to account for their righteousness and charity. Like us, they will be assigned their eternal glory based on how that judgment works out for them.

So, one must wonder, could God have made life on earth easier than He did on those other worlds? I mean, maybe God's children assigned to earth are His favorites and He wanted us to have an easier time of mortal life. Maybe God can play favorites . . . but I don't think so. The final judgment must be just. If all of God's children are going to be judged by the same final judgment, then the lives of those on all of God's planets must have similar challenges and difficulties. Thus, the rules of earth are almost assuredly the rules of many other worlds as well. We are not alone in this universe, but I cannot imagine a universe where standards of obedience shift depending on your location in it. I often wonder how those other worlds are doing and if they make as many mistakes as we do here on our planet. In any case, the reasons our very distant cousins were born on their planet are certainly the same reasons that we were born on ours. We will examine these shared reasons in the next chapter.

CHAPTER 2

LEARNING WISDOM VERSUS CHOOSING RIGHTEOUSNESS

PERHAPS THE BEST EXPLANATION of earth life may be found in comparing it to the first day of college. New students arrive for their first day of orientation in, let's say, Economics 101. A bearded, elderly professor lays out the schedule of lectures, labs, study groups, and exams. One overwhelmed coed, clearly having a different idea of what college was supposed to be like, plaintively asks, "But what about having fun?"

"Oh," the professor explains, "you are welcome to have fun wherever you can find it, but remember your real purpose in college is to *learn*. With each quiz and exam, you will be judged on how well you are learning. As you gain knowledge, you are welcome to enjoy the fellowship, football games, and other activities we have here."

So it is with earth life. We are here to learn, as the scriptures repeatedly explain. This overarching goal has been in place since the Garden of Eden. The forbidden fruit may have been "good for food" and "pleasant to the eyes," but that is not why it was eaten. Adam and Eve partook of the fruit because they wanted to understand earth life, "knowing good and evil" (Genesis 3:5–6).

In 2 Nephi 2:25, we learn that man is that he might have joy, but the Lord wants this joy to be based on knowledge, understanding, and wisdom. A fool can be happy. The naïve and uninformed can be content in their ignorance, but your Father in Heaven wants you to be joyful with a full understanding of the universe and its purpose. "Oh ye simple, understand wisdom: and, ye fools, be ye of an understanding heart" (Proverbs 8:5).

One would expect to find numerous teachings in the scriptures about finding joy and happiness. After all, "Men are, that they might have joy" (2 Nephi 2:25). But if we are on earth to learn, we would expect to find even more scriptures about gaining knowledge and wisdom. Though admittedly not an acceptably academic approach, if you run a word search in your electronic scriptures, you will find the following number of scriptural references for each word given below.

Joy: 403

Happiness: 82

Fun: 0

Pleasure: 93

Total number of references to attaining joy: 578

Learn: 168

Teach: 322

Knowledge: 380

Wisdom: 409

Total number of references to gathering wisdom: 1279

The scriptures mention finding knowledge over twice as often as finding joy. God wants us to find both, but He insists that our joy be based on knowledge of the gospel and our purpose here. Like college, our main purpose here on earth is to learn—while still enjoying our time here.

The Two Purposes of Life

To understand the foundation of the rules of earth, we have to understand why we are here. Obviously, we were sent here to obtain a body, but what are we supposed to *do* when we get here? I propose that we are here for two purposes, and to best understand them, we have to keep those reasons separate and distinct in our minds. Only one of them is mandatory, but both are necessary for our continued progression.

First, we were sent to Earth to *learn wisdom*. Many aspects of the world attest to this conclusion. For every action, there is a consequence, and from every consequence, we should learn something. Whether one lives a good life or bad, whether a person obeys the laws of the gospel or not, the purpose of learning wisdom is a requirement for all people living on earth. We must learn to walk, talk, work, and interact well with others. As citizens of Earth, we will all learn some wisdom while here. Some people will, of course, learn more than others.

Second, we were sent to earth to *choose righteousness*. For the many people who never have the chance to learn about the gospel in their lives, choosing righteousness may just mean continually trying to be a good, honest person. For those who are fortunate enough to learn about the gospel in this life, choosing righteousness will require obedience to a higher set of commandments. We will be judged for how we live our lives within the framework of our given time and place. Obviously, these two goals overlap a bit. It is hoped that we will learn wisdom, use that wisdom to choose righteousness, and that these righteous choices will give us more wisdom. We need to realize the difference between these two purposes and distinguish one from the other. In church talks and lessons, we heavily emphasize the goal of choosing righteousness, but by far, the majority of life's experiences are designed to teach us wisdom.

As Adam and Eve stood at the exit of the Garden of Eden, one has to wonder if they realized the importance of their next step. With that step, they put themselves on the path that was truly earth life. It was the first decision of many to come. If you think about it, almost every aspect of earth life is designed to encourage us to make choices—and then endure or enjoy the consequences of that choice. The following examples are provided to demonstrate that life is full of lessons to help you learn wisdom—if you just pay attention.

Learning the Wisdom of Caring for Your Body

My body is the most dedicated teacher I have ever had. It teaches me consequences for bad decisions all day, every day. For example, if I get up from my desk and decide not to watch my step, I can jam my foot into the desk leg. A consequence of that poor decision is that I will feel the immediate pain of a stubbed toe. I may even end up with a bruise bad enough to remind me many times throughout the coming days of my bad decision. Please note that my choice to step carelessly was not *unrighteous.* It was simply *foolish.* This immediate, painful reminder that I should tread more carefully gave me a little more wisdom. Thank you, desk leg. I might then limp into the kitchen to fix myself some lunch. I ignite the burner on the stove and heat up some soup. Perhaps not thinking clearly due to the pain in my toe, I pour the hot soup into a bowl too quickly, spilling some on my hand. The pain of the burn is immediate, chastising me for my haste. Again, my mistake was not unrighteous, but it was foolish, and I suffered the consequences. Thank you, hot soup.

Our bodies should be precious to us, and physical pain teaches us to take care of them. Painful reminders come in a variety of forms. I know I should get a good night's sleep. If I stay up too late at night, my body aches. I can't think clearly, and my eyes burn. I suffer exhaustion the next day. If I cut, bruise, or burn myself, the pain is acute and intense. I also know I should feed my body. When I skip meals, I develop hunger pains. My blood sugar plummets, and I become weak. My brain becomes obsessed with the thought of food. I also know my body has to eliminate waste products. If I forget to visit the restroom in a timely manner, I feel pain and pressure in the part of my body one would expect to ache in that situation. Pain is a punishment that increases to match our foolishness. As I ignore my need for sleep, food, drink, or a restroom break, my pain increases. I know I should keep my body warm. If I go outside on a winter's day without a coat, I get cold. If I ignore the chill, my exposed skin gradually flares in pain. If I continue to ignore the pain, I will develop frostbite, which will cause me pain for days to come. Similar consequences occur if I ignore the development of a sunburn. When I continue to ignore my body's communication, the consequences become more painful.

Your body is an amazing vehicle designed to help you stay alive. When your mind detects that you are in danger of severe injury or death, your adrenal glands emit the hormone adrenaline into your bloodstream to prepare your body to either flee or fight the danger. Your heart beats faster. Your respiration increases to make sure your muscles have all the oxygen they need to respond. Your mind becomes more alert and aware. "Adrenaline junkies" come to love this rush and seek it out by climbing mountain faces, kayaking dangerous rapids, skydiving, and participating in other similar activities. Only by flirting with danger and death can these thrill seekers experience the high of meeting challenges that can kill them. We may wonder about the common sense of adrenaline junkies. As long as they *balance their increased risk with increased care and attention*, they will probably be fine. If these athletes are wise enough to respect the dangers of their sport and take appropriate precautions, they can enjoy a lifetime of adrenaline rushes. If they are not wise enough to respect the increased danger, well, the consequence is severe for their misjudgment.

In a world of fast cars and impatient drivers, the consequences can be severe for carelessly driving to the store to buy bread and milk. In 2017, drunk, drugged, drowsy, and/or distracted drivers caused 40,000 deaths in the United States.[1] Those who fall into this category while they drive apparently do not respect the dangers of driving a two-ton car at sixty miles an hour. Learning that particular wisdom the hard way can come at the expense of people's lives.

By definition, the wisdom of caring for your body can mean being careful as you drive, pour soup, or free climb the side of a steep cliff. This wisdom also means keeping your body clean of known poisons, such as alcohol, tobacco, and opioids. Though the body's immediate rejection of these poisons is tempered over time, the cumulative effects are known to be destructive. It is no secret that drug abuse means you are abusing your body—not the drug. Pain comes with careless treatment of our bodies. Thus, the Word of Wisdom can be seen as an exhortation to learn wisdom without damaging your body to gain it.

Learning Wisdom from Others on How to Deal with Others

God gave us a body filled with millions of built-in nerve endings that teach us to care for it. The Lord wants us to develop other types of wisdom as well. After we learn to take care of ourselves, we also need to learn to care for other people. We start to develop our social ability as toddlers, and the task continues for the rest of our lives.

The first critically important relationship we develop is with our parents. They are our first authority figures. Parents have a serious responsibility in the future well-being of their children, as the scriptures remind us (D&C 68:25; 2 Nephi 4:6). Most parents do their best to give love, guidance, and discipline, a fact that they hope their children will appreciate as they become adults themselves. It is important for youth to have a good experience with their first authority figures since they will have to deal with many more in their future. As we grow, we establish relationships with our siblings, who are our first peers. Family establishes the foundation of our abilities to deal well with other people.

We go on to develop friendships with classmates, neighbors, and those with similar interests in sports, music, or theater. We learn the basics of social graces early in life. From the book, *All I Really Need to Know I Learned in Kindergarten*, we read,

> All I really need to know about how to live and what to do and how to be I learned in kindergarten. Wisdom was not at the top of the graduate-school mountain, but there in the sandpile at Sunday School. These are the things I learned: Share everything. Play fair. Don't hit people. Put things back where you found them. Clean up your own mess . . .[2]

As toddlers, we start to learn what is socially acceptable from our friends and family. Our bodies seem designed to help us communicate with others. For example, your sister has forty-three muscles in her face, which give her the capability of making hundreds of expressions of delight and approval at your kindness and thoughtfulness. She can use those same facial muscles to communicate to you emotions ranging from annoyance to unfettered rage at your selfish and rude behavior.[3] One should learn from those interactions how to better get along with others and avoid expressions of anger, whether from a sister or anyone else.

As we grow older, societal pressures to learn wisdom in dealing with other people increase. The consequences of not learning to respect our fellow man become more severe than a few disapproving looks. The rules and the consequences of not following them become apparent. A few of these societal laws and the consequences of breaking them are as follows:

1. Be sensitive to others' feelings (or risk being ostracized by your neighbors)
2. Develop good relationships with your coworkers (or be fired from your job)
3. Learn how to love, respect, and care for your spouse (or live a solitary life)

4. Be responsible in paying your bills (or lose the benefits of electricity, natural gas, and your home)
5. Respect and obey the laws of the land (or you will be thrown in jail)

Our penitentiaries are filled with men and women who didn't learn the wisdom of respecting the laws of their society and the rights of other people. This is another good example of the difference between learning wisdom and choosing righteousness. Prisoners are not in jail because they were unrighteous. They are in jail because they lacked the wisdom to obey the laws of their society.

Seek Knowledge and Gain Wisdom

Learning to care for your body and obey the laws of your society might be considered the very basics of the wisdom we must learn. As a people, we want to help our youth develop wisdom beyond that baseline, so schooling is both provided and required. School provides knowledge and wisdom that can be built upon that foundation. Numerous scriptures encourage us to gain both knowledge and wisdom. The Lord commanded Hyrum Smith to first obtain knowledge of His word before going out to preach it.

> Seek not to declare my word, but first seek to obtain my word, and then shall your tongue be loosed; then, if you desire, you shall have my Spirit and my word, yea, the power of God unto the convincing of men. But now hold your peace; study my word which hath gone forth among the children of men. (D&C 11:21–22)

Though not much is told to us about Jesus's childhood, adolescence, or early adulthood, the Savior's first thirty years of life were spent gathering knowledge and learning wisdom. The Apostle Luke, relating what Mary had told him about the Savior's early years, wanted to emphasize the importance of Jesus's education in His youth. He first summarizes, "And the child grew, and waxed strong in spirit, filled with *wisdom*: and the grace of God was upon Him" (Luke 2:40; italics added). Then Luke recounts the following story of the young Jesus's quest for knowledge.

As we know, on the return trip after a Passover celebration in Jerusalem, Joseph and Mary discovered that the twelve-year-old Jesus had gone missing. More than a little worried, the couple hurried back to Jerusalem to find Jesus in the temple "sitting in the midst of the doctors, both hearing them and asking them questions." I have heard this scene described as "the boy Jesus teaching in the temple," but this seems to be an incorrect summary of the scripture. Yes, for a twelve-year old boy, the priests and scribes may have been "astonished at his understanding and answers." But Jesus was there to learn, as he explained to his mother when she scolded him. "Wist ye not that I be about my Father's business?" (Luke 2:49). The Savior was gathering knowledge from these priests, not trying to teach or convert them. His own teaching ministry would not start for another eighteen years. A few verses later, Luke summarized the Savior's education yet a *third* time: "And Jesus increased in *wisdom* and stature, and in favour with God and *man*" (Luke 2:52; italics added).

Choosing Righteousness

Choosing righteousness comes after learning wisdom, because obviously you need a minimum level of knowledge to make your choices. The most basic rules of righteousness overlap with the laws of living in a society. As mentioned, prisons are filled with men and women who chose to be unrighteous in ways that were also illegal. But the line between unrighteous and illegal is sometimes blurred. For example, of the Ten Commandments, only number six (Thou shalt not kill), number eight (Thou shalt not steal), and sometimes number nine (Thou shalt not bear false witness) are illegal. There are numerous ways to be unrighteous without breaking civil law. On the other hand, righteous choices can sometimes break the laws of the land. To escape King Herod's edict designed to kill the young Jesus, Joseph and Mary fled Nazareth, making them fugitives of the law. The Founding Fathers of the fledgling United States carried out a rebellion that was clearly illegal in the view of the government of Great Britain.

Examples of the interaction of learning wisdom and choosing righteousness can be found in several scriptures. One of the most interesting can be found in one of the Savior's parables:

> Therefore whosoever heareth these sayings of mine, and doeth them, I will liken him unto a wise man, which built his house upon a rock: And the rain descended, and the floods came, and the winds blew, and beat upon that house; and it fell not: for it was founded upon a rock. And every one that heareth these sayings of mine, and doeth them not, shall be likened unto a foolish man, which built his house upon the sand: And the rain

> descended, and the floods came, and the winds blew, and beat upon that house; and it fell: and great was the fall of it. (Matthew 7:24–27)

The Lord likens following his teaching to a wise man who was smart enough to build his house upon the sturdy foundation of rock. Please note that the Lord does *not* tell us if this wise man was righteous. He tells us just that he had made a good decision. The Lord likens the man who does not follow His counsel to a foolish man (but not necessarily an unrighteous man) who was witless enough to build his house upon the ever-shifting sands. It was a bad decision, and there was a severe consequence. The take-away message of the parable is, "Be wise enough to choose righteousness and follow the teachings of the Savior."

As we gain wisdom, we may recognize that righteous choices are often illogical. The Good Samaritan risked his own life and spent time and money on a complete stranger (Luke 10:30–35). It was more than a little crazy for Ammon and his brothers to go on a mission to the Lamanites for fourteen years (Alma 17:4). Being honest, paying tithing, and serving others rarely helps us build our own personal fortunes. Only *if we find the greater good in helping others*—and how it improves our own character—does charity make sense.

Being Christlike does not mean that you must be naïve or overly trusting, as many people seem to believe. In gaining wisdom, we need to be able to see the world as it is. Otherwise, we leave ourselves open to robbers, scam artists, and physical harm. When the Savior sent his twelve Apostles forth to preach to Israel, he exhorted them, "Behold, I send you forth as sheep in the midst of wolves: be ye therefore wise as serpents, and harmless as doves" (Matthew 10:16). In his book *Jesus the Christ*, James E. Talmage summarizes the meaning of their instruction:

> The apostles were told to be prudent, to give no heedless offense, but to be wise as serpents, and harmless as doves . . . They were not to recklessly entrust themselves to the power of men; for wicked men would persecute them, seek to arraign them before councils and courts, and to afflict them in synagogues.[4]

While we should look for the best in people and remain charitable, wisdom demands we be aware of the dangers in doing so.

But whether we choose well or poorly, we learn from our judgments. As expressed by Orson Whitney and quoted by Spencer Kimball in *Faith Precedes a Miracle*,

> No pain that we suffer, no trial that we experience is wasted. It ministers to our education, to the development of such qualities as patience, faith, fortitude, and humility. All that we suffer and all that we endure, especially when we endure it patiently, builds up our characters, purifies our hearts, expands our souls, and makes us more tender and charitable, more worthy to be called the children of God . . . and it is through sorrow and suffering, toil and tribulation, that we gain the education that we come here to acquire and which will make us more like our Father and Mother in heaven.[5]

To take this idea to its extreme, I would like to consider my favorite verse in all the scriptures. It is poetic, deeply emotional, and teaches a great lesson. Joseph Smith had been in Carthage jail for three months, receiving news of the suffering of the Saints but not being able to help in any way. In frustration and anxiety for his friends and family, Joseph offers a prayer, asking where the Lord was hiding during this time and why He was not helping him or His Saints (D&C 121:1–6). In a letter dated ten days later, Joseph gives us a part of the revealed answer:

> And if thou shouldst be cast into the pit, or into the hands of murderers, and the sentence of death passed upon thee; if thou be cast into the deep; if the billowing surge conspire against thee; if fierce winds become thine enemy; if the heavens gather blackness, and all the elements combine to hedge up the way; and above all, if the very jaws of hell shall gape open the mouth wide after thee, know thou, my son, that all these things shall give thee experience, and shall be for thy good. (D&C 122:7)

First please note that there is no scriptural or historical evidence that the Lord arranged for Joseph Smith to be arrested and jailed at Liberty. This incarceration was the work of evil men who wanted to evict the Mormons from their state. Though God did not cause the arrest or incarceration, He still wanted Joseph to learn from it. This is true of every bad thing that happens in our lives. God does not plan, initiate, or engineer our difficult times. He knows troubles will come anyway (Matthew 6:34). The only good that can come out of such evil is the knowledge we gain from it. Likewise, I don't cause the strife in my children's lives, and I cannot protect them from it. I just hope they learn the patience, humility, and confidence that can come from coping with such issues.

On a side note, this verse illustrates the Lord's confidence in Joseph Smith. If Joseph had allowed the extreme difficulties that he suffered in Liberty jail to cause him to run away from his duties as prophet, those challenges would have decidedly *not* been for his experience and good. Since God knew Joseph would not turn away from his calling, He assured Joseph that his time in a cramped jail cell would give him experience (along with wisdom, patience, and other virtues) and he would be a better man because of it.

So, the first mission of earth life is to help your spirit learn wisdom. You are given a body that teaches you to care for it by administering pain for falls, burns, and other missteps. You were put into a society that teaches you to follow its rules about getting along with others. You go to school to learn knowledge and, we hope, the wisdom that can come with it. With that wisdom, you choose righteousness. Obviously, men have had varying levels of success in these endeavors. Many people on the earth are knowledgeable but not wise enough to be righteous. Other children of God are righteous but have made many foolish and painful choices. In the end, we all strive to acquire wisdom and apply that wisdom to making good choices.

Confusing Learning Wisdom and Choosing Righteousness

It is common to confuse the "learning wisdom" side of our lives with the "choosing righteousness" side of our lives. I have heard many prayers in which the Lord was asked to apply the *spiritual* blessings resulting from our righteousness to our *secular* lives of meeting the challenges of earth. It is as if we, because of our righteous choices, think we can choose the rewards we will receive through those choices. That's not the way it works, as the Lord explains in the scriptures:

> There is a law, irrevocably decreed in heaven before the foundations of this world, upon which all blessings are predicated—And when we obtain any blessing from God, it is by obedience to that law upon which it is predicated. (D&C 130:20–21)

We are often disappointed in God when righteousness does not translate into an easier life. Our logic seems to be that church and temple attendance, paying tithing, being honest, and serving others should allow us to accumulate points that can be used when praying for help in overcoming any challenge in our lives, be it physical, financial, or familial. If we are righteous, we often think we should be blessed with good health. If we attend church each Sunday, we feel we should be protected the other six days of the week.

Though difficult, we need to realize that the "gaining wisdom" part of our earthly lives continues throughout our time here. Choosing righteousness is noteworthy and laudable, but we should not think that righteous choices can be "cashed in" for exemptions from the challenges of life. This idea hearkens back to the refuted premise of Job that God always blesses the righteous with good health and good luck. As C. S. Lewis explained it:

> When a man turns to Christ and seems to be getting on pretty well (in the sense that some of his bad habits are now corrected), he often feels that it would now be natural if things went fairly smoothly. When troubles come along—illnesses, money troubles, new kinds of temptation—he is disappointed. These things, he feels, might have been necessary to rouse him and make him repent in his bad old days; but why now?[6]

We also need to realize that Earth will never stop presenting challenges, providing consequences, and thus teaching us wisdom—no matter how righteous we choose to be.

The Reasons for Earth Life

Though God should not be blamed for the difficulties in our lives, earth life really has to be a place of challenges. In truth, when we endure our hardships and tragedies well, we mature, develop empathy, and learn to handle grief. When we resist temptation, we increase our strength to continue to resist it. In creating the world, God did not want to have to continually invent new ways to challenge and prove us. God does not send random mishaps or disaster into our lives to help us develop inner strength, but He did build a healthy number of challenges into our earthly existence, many of them built on the fact that actions bring consequences.

Earth life was designed to be so challenging that God knew that if we survived long enough in it, we would have all the opportunities we would need to learn patience, long-suffering, empathy, and fortitude. We would have enough temptations to be able to prove our righteous desires and obedience. We would have enough interactions with our fellow man to learn charity, love, and caution. Life is like a boot camp for new recruits in the army. Boot camp is designed such that its young recruits will be trained, tested, and proven able to meet all the requirements of defending our country. Similarly, earth life provides us training and testing to see if we will prove worthy enough to be given responsibility and authority in the next life. There is no need for God to continually invent new hardships, temptations, or experiences for us. Earth life is daunting enough.

As a people, we know that the main reason for our sojourn on earth is to receive a body, use our agency, and prove ourselves able to navigate the perils of life. We want to do this righteously enough to gain our eternal reward, preferably in the celestial kingdom. Unless you refuse to get out bed tomorrow morning, you will get to make numerous choices that will affect your temporal comfort and/or your spiritual self. Such freedoms are often taken for granted. David O. McKay said,

> Next to the bestowal of life itself, the right to direct our lives is God's greatest gift to man. Freedom of choice is more to be treasured than any possession earth can give. It is inherent in the spirit of man. It is a divine gift to every normal being. . . . It is the impelling source of the soul's progress. It is the purpose of the Lord that man become like him. In order for man to achieve this, it was necessary for the Creator first to make him free. . . . Without this divine power to choose, humanity cannot progress.[7]

So, what is this earth life all about? As little children, we thought the worst thing earth life could bring upon us was bedtime or rain that ruined a family picnic. As adolescents, we came to the disturbing realization that life was more difficult than we first believed possible. As adults, we became aware of how dangerous the world can really be. There are dangers to our mortal bodies and dangers to our immortal spirits, but, we reason, isn't that why we have God? We pray to Him and He rescues us from perils and heartbreak, doesn't He? Well, yes and no.

In his book *Faith Precedes a Miracle*, Spencer W. Kimball lists a number of disasters and then asks,

> Could the Lord have prevented these tragedies? The answer is, Yes. The Lord is omnipotent, with all power to control our lives, save us pain, prevent all accidents, drive all planes and cars, feed us, protect us, save us from labor, effort, sickness, even from death, if he will. But he will not.[8]

Thus, President Kimball declares that, yes, the Lord can prevent all tragedy, but no, he will not. This declaration may seem a bit harsh. "Yes," we may think, "God cannot resolve every little challenge for us, but if it was a life-or-death situation that demanded a simple application of godly power to save the life of my loved one, couldn't He do so?"

THE GAME OF LIFE AND ITS RULES

I find it amazing that humanity has played the "Game of Life" for thousands of years, but we do not really seem to understand its rules. Latter-day Saints and other Christian religions believe that the world was created to provide humanity a place to live out their mortal lives. We believe we were sent here to receive a mortal body, to develop faith, and to learn obedience. So at least we have figured out the *goals* of living on earth, if not all the rules.

So what are the rules of living on earth? Did we have to do something to be born here? What governs where we are born or in what century we live? What dictates how and when we die? What are the reasons behind plagues, pestilence, famine, and war? We can't answer all these questions yet. To better understand our hardships, we need at least a basic understanding of the rules of earth. I believe these rules were a major part of the eternal plan that was presented to us in our premortal existence. The rules of agency and common consent would seem to require we be given some facts about Earth so we could make an informed decision about living here. Given the harshness of some of these rules, it also seems possible that they could have been a major point of contention that may have even contributed to the War in Heaven. In any case, if you are reading this text, then *you apparently agreed to those rules and signed up to come to earth*. That was an important decision, and you should appreciate that fact. At some point, you understood the need for a life on earth *and* you had faith in the plan of our Heavenly Father and Jesus Christ. Though you don't remember doing it, you agreed to the terms and realities of earth life, which is why you are here. Since the rules of earth are based on the premortal reasons for coming here, we should now discuss the premortal existence, where we agreed to be part of this earthly sojourn.

Chapter 3

The Premortal Existence

FOR A REVIEW OF THE RULES OF EARTH, we need to start at the beginning. For our purposes, that beginning is the premortal existence. In The Church of Jesus Christ of Latter-day Saints, we believe in a premortal existence where we lived as spirits before we were born on earth. There are several Biblical scriptures that speak of God choosing His prophets before the foundation of the earth (Jeremiah 1:5; Revelation 12:7–9; Ephesians 1:4; 2 Timothy 1:9). Thus, much of the rest of the Christian world believes in the doctrine of a premortal existence as well. Unfortunately, the Lord has told us little about that existence. This fact is not an oversight on His part. God hasn't told us much about the afterlife either. It seems apparent that He wants to focus on getting this life right, so we have little description of what the premortal existence was like.

To understand why tragedies and disasters occur here on earth, we need to review the reasons God wanted to have us live here in the first place. As Joseph Smith explained in *The History of the Church*,

> God himself, finding he was in the midst of spirits and glory, because he was more intelligent, *saw proper to institute laws* whereby the rest could have a privilege to advance like himself. The relationship we have with God places us in a situation to advance in knowledge. He has power to institute laws to instruct the weaker intelligences, that they may be exalted with Himself, so that they might have one glory upon another, and all that knowledge, power, glory and intelligence, which is requisite in order to save them in the world of spirits.[1]

God wanted us to have the opportunity to advance in knowledge, wisdom, empathy, and accomplishment. We had learned all that we could in the premortal existence. Our "childhood" there had run its course. It was time to move out of our dwelling with Heavenly Father and into a realm that would allow us to grow.

To better understand why God had us leave the premortal existence, we do not have to change our perception of God as a loving Heavenly Father. He is our Eternal Father. You may, however, have to change your perception of your own spiritual self. Don't think of yourself as a wide-eyed, eight-year-old being kicked out of the house. You were certainly naïve, but you were not a mere child. Think of yourself rather as a twenty-something, unemployed, single-adult spirit, living in your parent's basement and playing video games for most of the day. You have finished your schooling and seen all the sights of the premortal existence. You are bored and aimless. So, what does a loving Heavenly Father do? He sends you to the next phase of your existence. To that end, Heavenly Father and Jesus Christ executed the plan to create an earth where we could receive mortal bodies, develop faith, and learn obedience. As explained by Joseph Smith and then by Abraham,

> In the beginning, the head of the Gods called a council of the Gods; and they came together and concocted [prepared] a plan to create the world and people it.[2]

> Now the Lord had shown unto me, Abraham, the intelligences that were organized before the world was; and among all these there were many of the noble and great ones; And God saw these souls that they were good, and he stood in the midst of them, and he said: These I will make my rulers; for he stood among those that were spirits, and he saw that they were good; and he said unto me: Abraham, thou art one of them; thou wast chosen before thou wast born. And there stood one among them that was like unto God, and he said unto those who were with him: We will go down, for there is space there, and we will take of these materials, and we will make an earth whereon these may dwell; And we will prove them herewith, to see if they will do all things whatsoever the Lord their God shall command them; And they who keep their first estate shall be added upon; and they who keep not their first estate shall not have glory in the same kingdom with those who keep their first estate; and they who keep their second estate shall have glory added upon their heads for ever and ever. (Abraham 3:22–26)

At some point, creation of the world was initiated. Some of this planning and creative work is discussed in Genesis, Abraham, and Moses. Meanwhile, in the spiritual premortal realm, organization and teaching of those who were going to be Church leaders began. As Joseph F. Smith explained,

> I observed that they were also among the noble and great ones who were chosen in the beginning to be rulers in the Church of God. Even before they were born, they, with many others, received their first lessons in the world of spirits and were prepared to come forth in the due time of the Lord to labor in his vineyard for the salvation of the souls of men. (D&C 138: 55–56)

THE GRAND CONFERENCE IN HEAVEN

Once the planning for the creation had been accomplished, it was time to present the plan to all of God's children who would be born on earth for the next phase of teaching, testing, and advancement. One can only imagine that it would have been a large gathering indeed. Millions of spirits might have attended, all anxious to learn about their future. Any big change in one's life can be scary, and this would be one of the biggest changes to occur in our eternal lives. We needed information and a grand conference was called to give it to us.[3]

In actuality, we have little explanation of how the plan was presented at this gathering. We do know that, as summarized in the "The Family: A Proclamation to the World,"

> In the premortal realm, spirit sons and daughters knew and worshipped God as their Eternal Father and accepted His plan by which His children could obtain a physical body and gain earthly experience to progress toward perfection and ultimately realize their divine destiny as heirs of eternal life.[4]

To accept the plan, it had to be explained to us. In The Church of Jesus Christ of Latter-day Saints, we believe in the doctrine of common consent (D&C 26:2). New Church leaders and even new doctrine must be approved by Church membership (D&C 20:65). Common consent is linked to our agency, which was in effect in the premortal existence. So, drawing from how such meetings are run today, we might expect an explanation of what we were being asked to approve and support. It seems logical that the need for an earth life was first explained. We had reached a point in our development where we had to move from home to a new existence. We needed to be separated from our Heavenly Father. Only in mortal bodies, without our Father looking over our shoulders, could we prove that we would continue to do whatsoever the Lord commanded. As spirits with agency, we had to decide whether to agree to this separation.

It would seem incumbent upon our teacher to have explained to us that, as mortals on earth, mankind would have to choose this separation yet again. We would have been told that this second, confirming decision would occur in the Garden of Eden. Adam and Eve, as parents and proxies of all men and women, would make this choice for us. We were taught that the Lord would give Adam and Eve their options and the agency to make this landmark decision. Adam and Eve may not have understood all of the ramifications of their choice when they made it, but their choice would have been the same in any case. After all, there was no middle ground. They could choose earth life for their children or choose not to have children. The plan that had been established in the Grand Council in Heaven had to be followed. Adam and Eve, with the veil of forgetfulness about the premortal existence firmly in place, had to come to some earthly understanding of their choices and then make a decision. With that final decision, mankind would be separated from our Heavenly Father and placed on the earth.

THE EARTH EXPLAINED

Returning once again to the Grand Council training, a description of our future earth life would probably have continued. Once Adam and Eve had made the decision to accept earth life by symbolically partaking of the fruit of the tree of knowledge of good and evil (Genesis 3:12–13), mankind would start the process of leaving the premortal existence and being born on earth. Given the requirements of agency (understanding your options) and common consent (agreeing to the proposals of our leaders), I believe that we were told that the earth would be a vastly different place than the Garden of Eden. Since God cannot lie, I believe it was then explained to us that the Fall would most assuredly happen once Adam and Eve made the choice that they had to make. As with every choice, a consequence awaited, which is described in the third chapter of Genesis:

> And unto Adam he said, Because thou hast hearkened unto the voice of thy wife, and hast eaten of the tree, of which I commanded thee, saying, Thou shalt not eat of it: *cursed is the ground for thy sake*; in sorrow shalt thou eat of it all the days of thy life; Thorns also and thistles shall it bring forth to

> thee; and thou shalt eat the herb of the field; In the sweat of thy face shalt thou eat bread, till thou return unto the ground; for out of it wast thou taken: for dust thou art, and unto dust shalt thou return. (Genesis 3:17–19; italics added)

Thus it was declared that, after the Fall, the earth would bring forth "thorns and thistles," a term that is both literal and symbolic. From this decree came the first need to work. Unless men and women worked to remove them, weeds would choke out any herb or grain of the field. People would starve. Not only would the plant kingdom battle against Adam's efforts, so also would the animal kingdom. No longer would man live in peace with the animals as in the Garden of Eden. Man could now be hunted and slain by carnivores. Insects would afflict us. Viruses and bacteria would cause the death of millions. Earth's weather would turn against us. Sunny days and pleasant rains would be the norm. Drought, floods, tornadoes, and electrical storms would also occur, causing death and destruction of crops and livestock. In the spirit of full disclosure, we might have been taught that mortality meant that many of us would get sick from diseases or be killed by natural disasters long before the normal end of a full and natural life.

As spirit children, could we have actually understood what earth life would be like? Maybe not. We were almost certainly naïve about the harshness of such a world. Perhaps it was explained to us that all of this opposition to our happiness on earth was necessary for us to strive and learn. The goal behind this dangerous earth was that men would meet opposition and overcome it. We would have to battle weeds and insects. We would have to build our homes to withstand the barrages of weather. We would have to learn how to cure the diseases that would afflict us. We may have even been told it would take thousands of years to accomplish some of these tasks.

Against this backdrop of opposition in all things, we were told that we would also learn the commandments that God wanted us to obey while on earth. There would be commandments that govern how we worship God—prayer, Sabbath observance, respecting His name, following His Church leaders, etc. There would be commandments that govern how we treat each other—honoring our earthly parents, not stealing, killing only in defense of our home and family, and not lying to our neighbor or coveting his possessions. We would be held accountable for any transgression of these laws. We would also be expected to build a foundation of faith and establish our obedience on that base.

REUNITING WITH HEAVENLY FATHER—THE ATONEMENT

After hearing all about the dangers and responsibilities of earth, our congregation of pre-mortal spirits was probably ready to hear some good news. At this point, I would imagine that we were told about the Atonement. This would be our opportunity to return to live with our Heavenly Father. Through repentance, we could ask for forgiveness for our sins and, through the Atonement, be washed clean. Despite all the opposition the earth could throw at us, despite the sorrow that we would know, we would realize there was a light at the end of the tunnel. We would need to be obedient and stay humble enough to recognize our mistakes and repent of them. If we could do that, then we would be able to return to live with our Heavenly Father and our earthly family.

The Atonement was a wonderful gift, but it did have a couple of requirements. Obviously, we would need a Savior to carry out the Atonement. This Savior would have to be sinless, yet suffer mightily for all the sins of the world. It was a daunting task. The entire earthly plan depended on this Savior being successful in carrying out the required Atonement. Who would it be?

The book of Abraham picks up the account at this point:

> And the Lord said: Whom shall I send? And one answered like unto the Son of Man: Here am I, send me. And another answered and said: Here am I, send me. And the Lord said: I will send the first. And the second was angry, and kept not his first estate; and, at that day, many followed after him. (Abraham 3:27–28)

Joseph Smith added a few details to the history as well.

> At the first organization in heaven we were all present and saw the Savior chosen and appointed and the plan of salvation made, and we sanctioned it.
>
> The contention in heaven was—Jesus said there would be certain souls that would not be saved; and the devil said he would save them all, and laid his plans before the grand council, who gave their vote in favor of Jesus Christ. So the devil rose up in rebellion against God, and was cast down, with all who put up their heads for him.[5]

The Rebellion

As these scriptures relate, not everyone agreed with our Heavenly Father's plan. The leader of this group was Lucifer, the son of the morning (Isaiah 14:12). It soon became apparent that Satan had ulterior motives for his disagreement with the proposed plan.

As related in the Book of Moses,

> And I, the Lord God, spake unto Moses, saying: That Satan, whom thou hast commanded in the name of mine Only Begotten, is the same which was from the beginning, and he came before me, saying—Behold, here am I, send me, I will be thy son, and I will redeem all mankind, that one soul shall not be lost, and surely I will do it; *wherefore give me thine honor*. But, behold, my Beloved Son, which was my Beloved and Chosen from the beginning, said unto me—Father, thy will be done, and the glory be thine forever. Wherefore, because that Satan rebelled against me, and *sought to destroy the agency of man, which I, the Lord God, had given him, and also, that I should give unto him mine own power*; by the power of mine Only Begotten, I caused that he should be cast down; And he became Satan, yea, even the devil, the father of all lies, to deceive and to blind men, and to lead them captive at his will, even as many as would not hearken unto my voice. (Moses 4:1–4; italics added)

In our whole time in the premortal existence, why did Satan choose this moment to make his power grab? The following hypothesis is admittedly speculative, but it is seems logical. If Satan wanted to stage a coup, he would want to choose a time when the children of God were most unhappy and most scared of the future. Fear is a powerful motivator, and it seems likely that many of God's children might have been afraid that they would never be able to return to live again with their Heavenly Father. They could have feared that this planet Earth would expose them to dangers and temptations that they could not avoid or resist. Satan probably used that fear. Satan's proposal was that agency was not important to earth life and should be eliminated from the plan of redemption. If everyone would simply give up this whole idea of having freedom to choose, we could *all* make it back to live with Heavenly Father and our spiritual siblings. If no one could make errant choices, then no one's choice would ever be wrong. If we made no wrong choices on earth, then there would be no consequences, and we could all return to Heavenly Father. It is doubtful that Satan cared whether we had agency or not. He just wanted power, and agency could have been the campaign issue that he could exploit to that end. From the little we know about it, agency became the rallying point for the rebellion (Moses 4:3).

Satan probably even understood that agency *had* to be a key part of our earthly existence. After all, the whole point of God sending His spirit children to Earth was to "prove them herewith, to see if they will do all things whatsoever the Lord their God shall command them." Heavenly Father had to reject Satan's plan categorically.

Heartbreaking and ironically, a number of Heavenly Father's children decided to use their agency to rebel against agency.

> And it came to pass that Adam, being tempted of the devil—for, behold, the devil was before Adam, for he rebelled against me, saying, Give me thine honor, which is my power; and also a third part of the hosts of heaven turned he away from me because of their agency; And they were thrust down, and thus came the devil and his angels. (D&C 29:36–37)

There are consequences to bad decisions. In this verse and Revelation 12:4, we learn that this "third part of the hosts of heaven" was cast out because of their rebellion. We don't know how many of our spiritual brothers and sisters actually made this ill-fated decision, but one does have to wonder about them. In many Sunday School classes about the War in Heaven, this group of rebels is often portrayed as either inherently evil or incredibly gullible for following Satan. Were they simply the "overly-cautious" part of our Heavenly Father's children who did not want to risk failing to return to live with Heavenly Father? Or were they the "overly-ambitious" part of our spiritual brethren who wanted the same kind of power sought after by Satan? I always thought it strange that Satan could have gained followers in a rebellion based only on denying us our agency. No politician ever makes campaign promises that you *won't* get to make choices for yourself. Why would any of us want an earth life in which we are essentially slaves, not getting to make our own decisions?

We shall probably never know exactly what motivated Satan's followers, but it seems likely that the description of earth life would have been an important aspect of the rebellion. Descriptions of the challenges and pain of mortality must have strengthened the resolve of those who didn't want to participate in God's plan. Such a life, they may have thought, was just too hard. That attitude is, however, still alive and well here on earth. When listening to those who rant and rave about the unfairness, inequalities, and difficulties of life, one has to wonder why they didn't join the rebellion in the premortal existence when they had the opportunity.

The Veil of Forgetfulness

We don't, of course, remember the events of the Grand Council in Heaven, and I am making a few assumptions in its recounting. We don't remember the rebellion or even our individual decisions to come to Earth. This is because a "veil of forgetfulness" was placed over your mind at birth. It prevents you from remembering the initial orientation you were given about Earth as a spirit in the premortal existence. Life would indeed be much easier to understand if we could just remember our earlier existence. The veil was necessary for us to learn what needed to be learned and prove what needed to be proven. As Neil A. Maxwell put it:

> It seems clear, not only scripturally but logically, that this second estate could not include either the direct memories or the reference experiences of our first estate. If such were to impinge overmuch upon this second estate, our mortality would not be a true proving ground.[6]

Thomas S. Monson had similar feelings about the veil.

> How grateful we should be that a wise Creator fashioned an earth and placed us here, with a veil of forgetfulness on our previous existence, so that we might experience a time of testing, an opportunity to prove ourselves and qualify for all that God has prepared for us to receive.[7]

One of the requirements of building a world of faith is that *we do not have our memories about the premortal existence.* If we remembered our premortal experiences, at the very least we would know to expect an afterlife. We would obey God's commandments for all the wrong reasons. So that mortality would be a true proving ground, a veil was placed over our minds at birth, and we forgot about our previous estate.

With that veil of forgetfulness still over our minds, how do we determine the rules of earth? We will not be able to answer all the questions that exist regarding earth life. To better understand the mysteries of tragedy and disaster, we can look at our earth's history for clues. After all, the rules that govern tragedies have been in place for the thousands of years of recorded earth history. All of man's calamities and hardships inherent to earth life *had* to follow those initial rules. By observing the tragedies of earth's recorded history, we may be able to determine the rules that govern them.

For example, if no one ever told you the rules of American football, you might be confused as you watched your first several games. The play would seem chaotic, with players running into each other and referees penalizing teams for the strangest wrongdoings. But if you watched enough football, weekend after weekend, you would eventually come to understand each rule and penalty as well as someone who has played the game since childhood. In essence, I suggest that we can do much the same thing to figure out the rules of earth. If we look at enough world history, where the rules of earth life have been in effect for millennia, we can develop a basic understanding of the laws that govern our mortal existence. Life is a much harder game to understand than football. If we observe enough of earth's history, we can at least have some insight into its rules.

The rules of earth were established—and possibly explained to us—in the premortal existence. God cannot lightly set aside the rules upon which our mortal existence was founded—not for the earth as a whole nor for you as an individual. To illustrate this fact, the next several chapters will identify a few of the rules of earth. Then, to emphasize the importance of each rule, we will review the times in Earth's history when their enforcement would have been the most difficult for God.

Chapter 4

Rule 1: The Earth Must Be a Place of Faith

THE FIRST RULE OF EARTH is also the requirement that most limits what God can do for His petitioners. Despite all His powers, God has to constantly hide them away from public view. This mortal existence must be a place of faith. As Alma explained in Alma 32, we are to labor to convert our faith into knowledge. However, we cannot get that knowledge without first dedicating ourselves to the effort and learning the obedience that will be required to obtain it. If God makes Himself known, or if people even see His angels in action, then they will have gained knowledge of God's existence without the spiritual relationship that should develop with it. This simply cannot be.

The encouragement to "have faith" is so common and overused that it has become a cliché. Faith is the first principle of the gospel. We learn about it at such an early age that we really don't appreciate how hard it is for the Lord to maintain it on the earth. Even Joseph Smith forgot the rule that the earth has to be a place of faith. After several months in Liberty Jail, Joseph approached the Lord with a heartfelt petition to help the Church in its time of need.

> O God, where art thou? And where is the pavilion that covereth thy hiding place? How long shall thy hand be stayed, and thine eye, yea thy pure eye, behold from the eternal heavens the wrongs of thy people and of thy servants, and thine ear be penetrated with their cries? Yea, O Lord, how long shall they suffer these wrongs and unlawful oppressions, before thine heart shall be softened toward them, and thy bowels be moved with compassion toward them? O Lord God Almighty, maker of heaven, earth, and seas, and

> of all things that in them are, and who controllest and subjectest the devil, and the dark and benighted dominion of Sheol—stretch forth thy hand; let thine eye pierce; let thy pavilion be taken up; let thy hiding place no longer be covered; let thine ear be inclined; let thine heart be softened, and thy bowels moved with compassion toward us. Let thine anger be kindled against our enemies; and, in the fury of thine heart, with thy sword avenge us of our wrongs. Remember thy suffering saints, O our God; and thy servants will rejoice in thy name forever. (D&C 121:1–6)

Joseph is not asking the Lord to give general blessings to the Church membership. Joseph had reached the conclusion that the Church was in such dire need that God needed to break out of His hiding place to set things right and avenge the Church of its enemies. In his attempt to persuade, Joseph reminds God that He is the Creator of heaven and earth and that Satan and his realm are still subject to Him. Joseph's frustration that God continued to hide His power is evident. This quote is more of a challenge to God to appear in His power and glory as it is a prayer. As so many of God's children have done throughout history, Joseph pled with God to demonstrate His power and strike down his oppressors.

God reassures Joseph that the persecutors of the Church would receive their punishments—but not necessarily in this life. The world had to remain a world of faith, both in 1839 and still today. As much as it pained Him, God could not yet come out of his pavilion and hiding place.

> Wo unto all those that discomfort my people, and drive, and murder, and testify against them, saith the Lord of Hosts; a generation of vipers shall not escape the damnation of hell. Behold, mine eyes see and know all their works, and I have in reserve a swift judgment *in the season thereof*, for them all; For *there is a time appointed* for every man, according as his works shall be. (D&C 121:24–25; italics added)

D&C 121 is a beautifully written prayer between Joseph (verses 1–6) and God (verses 7–46). The Lord comforts Joseph and encourages him, but He does not agree to give Joseph the show of godly power and revenge he requested. From the ancient days of the Roman persecution of Christians, through the mob's abuse of the Saints in Missouri, and still today, faithful Christians like Joseph Smith have pled with God to reveal His power. After all, to stop any of these persecutions would require only a small task force of angels to put things right. Is that too much to ask? How could God allow the atrocities of persecutions without stepping in and stopping the abuse? In the face of violence and murder of faithful innocents (Alma 14:8), couldn't He set aside the need for a world of faith for a moment? The entire purpose for us coming to Earth rests on the foundation that we will learn obedience and wisdom through faith. In the history of the earth, there are only a few occasions so desperate that God has superseded the need to restrain this power and risk detection.

There are, of course, a small number of people, called prophets or seers, who do get to see God and talk to Him. God needs His prophets on earth, and occasionally He needs to have a face-to-face meeting with one of them. But notice that these visits were never public appearances. Moses had to turn aside into the wilderness of Mount Horeb to see the burning bush (Exodus 3:1–3) and then go to the top of a mountain to get the Ten Commandments (Exodus 19:20). Only Peter, James, and John saw the Savior meet with Moses and Elijah on the Mount of Transfiguration (Mark 9:2–4). Only Paul saw the Savior on the road to Damascus (Acts 9:7). Joseph Smith was by himself in the woods near Palmyra when he saw God the Father and Jesus Christ (Joseph Smith—History 1:14). Even in appearing to His servants, the Lord minimizes the possible damage of having other people see Him.

The best definition of faith that I have found is given in Alma.

> And now, as I said concerning faith—faith is not to have a perfect knowledge of things; therefore if ye have faith ye hope for things which are not seen, which are true. (Alma 32:21)

The best explanation that the world must remain a place of faith is given in the same chapter, just a few verses earlier.

> Yea, there are many who do say: If thou wilt show unto us a sign from heaven, then we shall know of a surety; then we shall believe. Now I ask, is this faith? Behold, I say unto you, Nay; for if a man knoweth a thing he hath no cause to believe, for he knoweth it. And now, how much more cursed is he that knoweth the will of God and doeth it not, than he that only believeth, or only hath cause to believe, and falleth into transgression? (Alma 32:17–19)

Thus if a man named Bill sees a sign from heaven, he will *know* there is a God there. Faith is no longer needed, and the design of Bill's mortal existence is foiled. Even worse, with that new-found knowledge, Bill now has an increased responsibility to do the will of God. Unfortunately, Bill did not gain his knowledge with the lifetime of effort and spiritual dedication usually required for it. If he remains unprepared to do the will of the Father, despite seeing a sign, then Bill is cursed. In the words of the Savior, "For unto whosoever much is given, of him shall be much required." (Luke 12:48)

But in a review of the scriptures, it appears God has been generally successful at calling prophets and other Church leaders who were ready to make a higher commitment to Him. Moses and other Old Testament prophets were faithful in carrying out their callings. In the Book of Mormon, the brother of Jared talked with the pre-mortal Jesus Christ face-to-face and continued faithful (Ether 6:17). Peter, James, John, and Paul were also dedicated servants. The several generations of Nephites who saw Jesus Christ descend from the sky and heard Him teach maintained peace in the land and love in their hearts their entire lives (4 Nephi 1:18). Joseph Smith was valiant until his death, as have been all the prophets since. This is not to say that men who see great miracles cannot fall away. All three witnesses to the Book of Mormon—Oliver Cowdery, David Whitmer, and Martin Harris—left the Church after seeing an angel and hearing God's voice. Other men may have received miraculous calls from God but did not respond. We simply don't know about them, because, by not responding, they simply slid away into obscurity.

LINE UPON LINE

In His mercy, the Lord has arranged that we learn about Him in stages. That is why we start with faith. Faith includes enough doubt that we have a reason or excuse for our waywardness. The doubt inherent in faith gives men time to find their way. Faith allows men to learn wisdom and realize they should choose righteousness. As a man develops faith, he has time to grow closer to God, without having to live at the level of commitment a perfect knowledge would require.

Because of the importance of the concept, the scriptures explain this concept in many different ways. Isaiah used the "line upon line, precept upon precept" explanation in his teachings (Isaiah 28:9–10). Nephi used the same catchy phrase in the Book of Mormon, as did the Lord in the Doctrine and Covenants.

> For behold, thus saith the Lord God: I will give unto the children of men line upon line, precept upon precept, here a little and there a little; and

> blessed are those who hearken unto my precepts, and lend an ear unto my counsel, for they shall learn wisdom; for unto him that receiveth I will give more; and from them that shall say, We have enough, from them shall be taken away even that which they have. (2 Nephi 28:30)

> For he will give unto the faithful line upon line, precept upon precept; and I will try you and prove you herewith. (D&C 98:12)

In the Gospels of the Bible, the Lord told the people to "take heed what ye hear," because once you hear it, you will be responsible for it. Those who want to know the gospel (if you have ears to hear), listen and learn, and you will be given even more.

> And he said unto them, Take heed what ye hear: with what measure ye mete, it shall be measured to you: and unto you that hear shall more be given. (Mark 4:24)

> Take heed therefore how ye hear: for whosoever hath, to him shall be given; and whosoever hath not, from him shall be taken even that which he seemeth to have. (Luke 8:18)

> He that hath ears to hear, let him hear. (Matthew 11:15)

The metaphor of comparing basic doctrine to milk and deeper doctrine to meat seems to have appeared in the days of the New Testament. Paul laments that the Corinthians and the Hebrews were too carnal to be taught more than the milk of the gospel. Obviously, he wishes his congregations were learning doctrinal truths.

> And I, brethren, could not speak unto you as unto spiritual, but as unto carnal, even as unto babes in Christ. I have *fed you with milk, and not with meat*: for hitherto ye were not able to bear it, neither yet now are ye able. For ye are yet carnal: for whereas there is among you envying, and strife, and divisions, are ye not carnal, and walk as men. (1 Corinthians 3:1–3; italics added)

> For when for the time ye ought to be teachers, ye have need that one teach you again which be the first principles of the oracles of God; and are become such as have *need of milk, and not of strong meat.* For every one that useth milk is unskilful in the word of righteousness: for he is a babe. But *strong meat* belongeth to them that are of full age, even those who by reason of use have their senses exercised to discern both good and evil. (Hebrews 5:12–14; italics added)

The Lord Himself uses this same metaphor in the Doctrine and Covenants in His directions to Martin Harris on how to preach.

> And I command you that you preach naught but repentance, and show not these things unto the world until it is wisdom in me. For *they cannot bear meat now, but milk they must receive*; wherefore, they *must not know these things, lest they perish*. (D&C 19:21–22; italics added)

In these earliest days of the restored Church, why did the Lord tell Martin Harris that the world "must not know these things [the meat of the gospel] lest they perish"? Because if they were taught the meat of the gospel, the people would be required to live a life in accordance with these higher laws. In the Lord's opinion, the people could not have lived up to those requirements and thus would have perished.

Faith and Creation

It would be hard to overstate the amount of work the Lord has had to do to maintain this earth as a world of faith. It started with the Creation. Since the publication of Charles Darwin's book *The Origin of the Species*, the debate has raged between Creationists and Evolutionists. Fueled by the controversy, every science possible—astronomy, geology, microbiology, botany, genetics, etc.—has examined our earth, fossils, and now DNA for evidence of God's hand. These scientists have found the natural, evolutionary processes used to create a world of life. Evidence of Earth's botanical and zoological history have been discovered in the rock layers that were once layers of sediment under oceans and lakes. Genetics analysis is doing much the same thing today by analyzing DNA and determining how each species came to be.

In order to maintain the world of faith, God had to "hide His tracks" for millions of years. The creation of the universe, the earth, life, and mankind had to be done in such a way that man could doubt or deny that God had any role in the process. Throughout history, God has had to answer prayers in such a way that men could not prove that God was behind the blessings. I have heard testimonies from Church members who claim that they recently had an experience that absolutely proves that God exists and personally answers their prayers. I appreciate the zeal of their testimonies, but if someone really had an experience that proves God's existence, then God has failed to maintain our world of faith. I don't believe that to be true. God has done this for a long time, so I have to believe He is really good at it.

Thus God has to restrain Himself such that His answers to prayer and His blessings all have a rational explanation behind them other than divine intervention. I think the greatest challenge of being a God would be to *not* do miracles. When Satan was tempting the Savior in the wilderness, he challenged Him to prove He was God by performing miracles (Matthew 4:3–7). When the Savior was on the cross, observers, chief priests, scribes, elders, and even the two thieves crucified beside him challenged Him to miraculously come down from the cross (Matthew 27:39–44). It seems everyone wants God to prove Himself by doing miracles.

We have the accounts of the miracles accomplished by the Savior in the letters of Matthew, Mark, Luke, and John, but the burden of proof is high to convince anyone of a miracle. The witnesses of four uneducated men from over two millennia ago is certainly not enough evidence to conclude that Jesus Christ is our Savior. Such an epiphany requires spiritual confirmation for those willing to seek it.

PROOF BY STATISTICS

There are two types of data that one can use to argue for the existence of God. The first type is spiritual data. This data is made up of the spiritual witnesses that Christians have received and testified of throughout their lives. Your personal spiritual data—stirrings and assurances that you feel of the Holy Ghost as you pray, read your scriptures, or attend church—is the evidence behind your testimony. But spiritual data, however real it is to each individual, cannot be documented or verified. Thus, though the testimonies of God may number in the millions, they cannot be used to scientifically prove anything. The sciences only accept physical data that can be documented and proven. When all the physical data is collected, it then has to be sifted by statistics to prove that our proposed hypothesis and conclusions are supportable.

Merriam-Webster defines statistics as "a branch of mathematics dealing with the collection, analysis, interpretation, and presentation of masses of numerical data."[4] Statistics can be used for anything. Its methods are used extensively in sports to describe the abilities of teams and individual players. Statistics are used in science to determine if a given hypothesis is supportable by the data to form a defensible conclusion. But statistics have not yet been able to prove that God exists. This failure is not due to a lack of trying. If you Google the concept, you will quickly find yourself falling down the rabbit hole of bizarre claims, counter-claims, and rude blog posts. Myriads of people have claimed to be able to scientifically or mathematically prove God's existence, but no credible, defensible study has done so. Could a scientific study and statistics be used to prove God's existence and thus change our world from being a place of faith?

To illustrate the difficulties that God has in maintaining this earth as a place of faith, let me propose a possible study. I would like to determine if religious people who are active in their church are more blessed than non-religious people. Blessings can come in a number of forms, so let us first define the word "blessing" to mean longer lives and higher incomes. (Some may argue that blessings should include whether churchgoers live *happier* lives. While I would love to include happiness as a measure of blessings, without a happiness meter, I cannot accurately and definitively quantify happiness. We have to compare what can be measured.)

So, through interviews and research, I have two hypotheses I wish to investigate: Is it true that actively religious people live longer than non-religious people? Do actively religious people make higher incomes than non-religious people? Now I need to structure my study and limit my independent variables as much as possible. First, I am going to limit my sampling of religious and non-religious people to the states of Colorado, Idaho, and Utah. These three states have similar weather, population, economic health, and lifestyles. Second, I want to limit my sampling to people who are essentially living the Word of Wisdom. Anyone who smokes, drinks heavily, or indulges in drugs is going to shorten his or her life and probably limit his or her career path. Blessings from living healthy lifestyles come to anyone who lives a healthy lifestyle, religious or not. So, we have to remove that variable from our study of specific blessings.

With my parameters now established, I begin my study. I want as large a sample size as possible since my statistics and conclusions get stronger with larger data sets, so I interview thousands of adults who live a healthy lifestyle in my selected states. I set up a database of those who are within my parameters and keep track of their reported incomes. I follow these same people for years and record their exact ages at death.

After decades of data collection, I then take my spreadsheet and apply my statistics to it. I run what is called the "unpaired t-test" on my data. This analysis will compare the average age of death and the average incomes of our two selected populations. In doing so, the t-test will consider the spread of the data, or variance, of each group. The larger the variance, the further apart the averages have to be to support the conclusion that the two groups are statistically different from each other.[2, 3] The t-test is designed to look for slight differences in the averages between two populations. If a difference is there, this statistic will flush it out.

In actuality, this study would be hard to accomplish, and I don't have the financial means, the time, or the inclination to take on such a task. Though I have not run such a study, other statisticians in the health sciences, insurance industry, and financial markets are running similar investigations (though for different reasons than to prove God exists). *So if God blessed His actively religious followers with physical blessings above and beyond those of His non-religious children, some statistician would eventually notice.* The results would be published—and it would become front-page news. Headlines would announce that "God Exists!" and "Go to Church to Make More Money and Live Longer!" Why would this be a problem, you might ask?

The Church of Jesus Christ of Latter-day Saints has an active missionary program. We love having new people join the Church, but we instruct our missionaries that we want investigators to join the Church because they are spiritually converted. We don't want people joining the Church because they have proof that by doing so they will be financially richer or enjoy a longer life span. Thus, God has established His Church on the foundation of faith, which requires a spiritual conversion, rather than on knowledge, which does not. To accomplish this aim, God has to temper His physical blessings so that not even the statisticians can discover them.

A Statistical Study of Prayer

You may wonder about my statement that God's presence can never be statistically proven. Though my suggested study has never been run, there have been studies that have tried to prove God's existence. One of the largest of such studies was designed to answer the question if prayer works. The study was concluded in 2006, cost $2.4 million, and was published in the prestigious *American Heart Journal.*[4] This study was designed to prove the hypothesis that prayer would help patients recover from heart bypass surgery with fewer complications. For the study, arrangements were made such that members of several religious congregations across the country prayed for specific patients within the study. They were to pray for these patients by name and ask "for a successful surgery with a quick, healthy recovery and no complications." A population of 1,800 patients who were to undergo coronary bypass surgery were divided into three groups. One group of patients had *no* prayers offered for them, at least by the religious congregations in the study. The second group of patients *did* have prayers offered up for them. Each patient in the group was informed that entire congregations were praying for them. The third group also had prayers offered for them, but they were told they may or may not be prayed for during the study. This last group was to control for a placebo effect. It was feared that those receiving prayers would report feeling better because, due to the prayers of others, they *believed* they should feel better.

After the statistics had been run, it was found that there was no difference in the rates of post-surgical complications between the three groups. The results were reported in the *New York Times* under the title "Long-Awaited Medical Study Questions the Power of Prayer."[5] At the end of the article, the leader of one of the prayer congregations stated that, "the research on prayer and spirituality is just getting started." Even so, I don't think other such studies will be successful either. The first rule of the rules of earth is that the earth must remain a place of faith. So God's blessings must remain mostly spiritual, because too many physical blessings of the righteous would be noticed. The Lord must keep His existence hidden such that only a sincere spiritual search will find Him.

Chapter 5

Rule 2: You Must Do Work

If you remember, the Garden of Eden was a sweet place to live. Apparently, there were orchards aplenty (Genesis 2:9). Adam was only commanded to "dress" the garden and keep it up. From later scriptures, it appears this would not have taken a whole lot of effort on Adam's part. Apparently, there were no weeds, since those only came later. Adam didn't even have to plant the trees (Genesis 1:29). Though he did not perform the labor, Adam was told, "Of every tree of the garden thou mayest freely eat" (well, *except* for the tree of the knowledge of good and evil). When Adam and Eve chose to eat the one fruit they were supposed to leave alone, the Fall occurred. Immediately the rules of earth became law, and everything changed. Eden, where food was readily and freely available, was no more. The Lord then explained to Adam the exact consequences of his decision. There would now be opposition to anything Adam endeavored to do.

> For it must needs be, that there is an opposition in all things. If not so, my firstborn in the wilderness, righteousness could not be brought to pass, neither wickedness, neither holiness nor misery, neither good nor bad. (2 Nephi 2:11)

Generally we interpret this verse to address the spiritual side of our lives. Righteousness is opposed by wickedness, happiness is opposed by despair, and truth by untruth. But this new law applied to much more mundane areas of life as well. The Lord explained that Adam would find opposition in just trying to feed himself.

> Cursed is the ground for your sake; in sorrow shalt though eat of it all the days of thy life. Thorns also and thistles shall it bring forth to thee; and thou shalt eat the herb of the field; in the sweat of thy face shalt thou eat bread, till thou return unto the ground. (Genesis 3:17–19)

So thorns and thistles would oppose Adam's efforts to raise his crops. Those weeds would be so tenacious that Adam would have to work hard enough to sweat from his labors.

Throughout history, Adam and Eve have been blamed for getting us kicked out of Eden, thus forcing mankind to work. This move was, of course, inevitable. Since the earth was a place to be tried and tested, opposition was a forgone conclusion. First, opposition had to be spiritual. Righteousness battles wickedness and so forth. But the opposition had to be temporal as well. Weeds, insects, rodents, and other wildlife would destroy our crops. Disease and carnivores would kill our herds. Eventually, man learned how to overcome most of these challenges, but the opposition remains. Most all of us still must do work.

We have numerous scriptures that remind us to not be slothful (Proverbs 12:24, Matthew 25:26, D&C 42:42). We are to work to feed our families. At one point Paul says it simply enough: "That any would not work, neither should he eat" (2 Thessalonians 3:10). We are to work to maintain our homes. In Ecclesiastes 10:18, we are reminded that "by much slothfulness the building decayeth; and through idleness of the hands the house droppeth through." We are to work in our profession as well. In Romans 12:11, Paul counsels the Saints to be "Not slothful in business; fervent in spirit; serving the Lord."

Work gives us something constructive to do with our time. Work gives us a sense of accomplishment at the end of a busy day. Besides learning how to be industrious and provide for our families, work teaches us another skill that is also important to the Lord. As crazy as it may sound, it appears that the earth teaches us skills of organization.

ORGANIZATION

We know that God did not create our earth out of nothing. The matter He used to build our solar system already existed in this region of space, so the creation could actually be better described as an organization (Abraham 4). Elements that were created in the interior of ancient suns were collected and put into place to make our earth and its moon. We believe that God has been organizing planets like ours for a very long time. If you consider the nature of work, it becomes apparent that He wants us to learn skills of organization as well.

In many creation accounts from ancient peoples around the world (including the Genesis version), the earth was created out of the midst of chaos. In a few such accounts, chaos actually takes on a sinister personality. This is an understandable conclusion. Chaos continually works to undermine and destroy organized societies. Weather, mold, and insects destroy our homes and habitats. Angry and evil men try to destroy the organized governments of those who oppose them. However, where you find chaos and anarchy, you also find the hungry and homeless. By commanding Adam and his children to work and provide for each other, God has commanded us to battle against destructive and disorganizing forces. Only organized societies can tend to the temporal needs of its population so it may then learn of spiritual matters.

When the Savior first started His ministry, He organized His Church upon the earth. He called His Apostles as Church leaders, taught the membership correct doctrine, and sent out missionaries (Matthew 4:18–23). When the Savior ended His ministry, He passed on to the spirit world and organized the missionary efforts there (D&C 138:30). He then visited the Americas and organized a church among the people of the Book of Mormon. Later, He organized the restored Church. If we look to the Savior as our example, we find that organization was a recurring theme in everything He did.

ENTROPY

Incredibly, even in the laws of physics, we find hints that the universe is focused on teaching its people to be organized. The second law of thermodynamics states that in any spontaneous reaction, "entropy" always increases. Entropy is a measure of disorder or randomness. In natural reactions, entropy always increases. If you drop a deck of cards, they will become disordered. If you make a meal for your family, the kitchen becomes disarrayed. Well-organized project plans in your workplace are soon beset by delays, cancellations, increased costs, and other disorganizing forces. Organization is the opposite of entropy. This is true if you are simply melting a crystal or monitoring levels of disorder in your family room. In fact, perhaps a comparison of the two is in order.

At minus 273 degrees centigrade, molecular motion stops. In a crystal at such low temperatures, atoms are lined up in perfect columns and rows. If the crystal is perfect, there is no disorder. Entropy is zero.[5] Such orderliness can be compared to your family room right after you have cleaned and vacuumed. Everything is in its place. Toys are concealed in the toy box. Even the throw pillows are positioned perfectly on the sofa.

When energy is applied to our frozen crystal, its temperature rises. Atoms start vibrating and then move out of their regimented order, bashing into one another, and spiraling away. Entropy increases. As our frozen crystal continues to heat up, it eventually makes the transition from being an orderly solid to a fluid, less-organized liquid. If we continue applying energy, the liquid becomes a disorderly gas, and its entropy goes through the roof.

Now let us return to the orderly family room and apply some energy into the space. That energy can be in the form of a blast of wind, a ball of fire, an active three-year-old, or a group of teenagers. In short order, toys are removed from the toy box. Used glasses and plates crowd the end tables. Shoes, socks, and video game controllers litter the floor. Random papers are stacked on the couch. Throw pillows have been thrown to the floor to assist in better viewing of the television. Entropy in this room has been increased by the application of the energy of family and friends. The room is, in summary, a mess.

Entropy can be reduced in only one way. Applying random energy to a crystal or a family room increases its entropy, but applying energy *under the control of a directing intelligence* will create order and decrease entropy. In the case of a dropped deck of cards, you have to pick up those cards and, allowing your mind to direct the energy in your hands, organize them into a nicely stacked deck. In the case of the evaporated crystal, we have to do work to concentrate the dispersed atoms and then cool them to freeze back into a solid. The disorderly family room will require experienced, controlled work to organize and clean. "A place for everything and everything in its place" can be applied to cleaning a room or creating a world. Organization helps families, businesses, church congregations, and governments be more efficient at providing for the well-being of each member.

If we define work as increasing organization in the face of entropy, we can see that any growing thing must do work to build and insert new cells. A growing plant uses the energy from sunshine to organize carbon dioxide into more plant tissue. My baby granddaughter consumes starches, sugar, protein, and fat. Using the chemical energy from the food itself, her infant body assembles the ingredients of her nourishment into more muscle, bones, and tissue to allow her growth. In both examples, DNA (or deoxyribonucleic acid) provides the directing intelligence behind this organization. DNA is our biological programming that is provided to every cell in our bodies. Fortunately, growth is a natural process that we don't have to consciously drive forward. Our bodies are constantly organizing so we can function and perform work on our environment. We too must learn organization just to keep ahead of a world that naturally drifts toward disarray.

Chapter 6

Rule 3: The Earth Is a Dangerous Place

Dr. Neil deGrasse Tyson is a famous astrophysicist, author, and the host of several television shows on astronomy. Because astrophysicists study the universe and its workings, Dr. Tyson is often asked about his belief in God. His response is that, in all his study of the cosmos, he has never found evidence of a benevolent being. He stated,

> If your concept of a creator is someone who is all-powerful and all-good . . . [when] I look at disasters that afflict Earth and life on Earth—volcanoes, hurricanes, tornadoes, earthquakes, disease, pestilence, and congenital birth defects . . . I just ask, "How do you deal with that?"[1]

Dr. Tyson is not alone in his conclusion. Many people look at the dangers of the earth and dismiss the concept of a loving God who would include so many dangers on our beautiful planet. The earth really is a beautiful planet. We have a warm sun, a blue sky, a beautiful moon, mountains, trees, flowers, and wildlife. We have plentiful air, water, and food. It is a wonderful place to live out our mortality. For 99 percent of the time, the weather is great, and living here is like an extended vacation.

But Dr. Tyson may not have considered in his complaint that we have not been placed on the earth to enjoy extended vacations. As stated earlier, we are sent to the earth to learn wisdom and choose righteousness. On a vacation world, the hardest decision we might have to make is whether we want to visit the mountains or the beach today. The only wisdom we might learn from that choice is that mountains can be rather cold this time of year. The earth was meant to be a place that challenges us at every turn. To bring out the best in us, or the worst, earth life had to put us under some stress. So, first and foremost, we were given bodies that need to be sheltered and fed almost continuously. Whether we spent our lives as hunter-gatherers, farmers, or office workers, we face the need to care for our families and ourselves every single day. We have to do that in the face of droughts, famine, sickness, and layoffs. We live in a world where consequences are generally more severe than getting a slight chill from the mountain air.

To understand this rule of earth, we need to examine the trials that have been put here and consider how they provide consequences to bad decisions. As we look at each of Earth's dangers, we can, it is hoped, appreciate what each is designed to do.

DANGER FROM THE BLESSINGS OF EARTH

Ironically, some of the most dangerous features of earth are also needed for us to survive. If we are careless and do not use wisdom in our actions, some of the most crucial components of earth life can actually kill us. These elements are an interesting example of the doctrine of "opposition in all things" since they are essential to life but threaten it as well.

GRAVITY

Obviously, we need gravity to hold us on the earth so we don't float into space. Gravity allows our feet and car tires to gain traction so we can move about from place to place. Obviously, we need this force working on us at all times for us to live a normal life. Incredibly, gravity never fails. Gravity will constantly pull you to the earth as you walk down the sidewalk, and it will pull you down just as assuredly if you carelessly step off a cliff. The harm done by gravity increases with the distance of the fall. In 2014 in the United States, 31,959 people died as the result of accidental falls.[2] All such falls were accidents that happened to someone standing on a cliff, a ladder, a rooftop, or another elevated platform and simply stumbled. Gravity teaches that the consequences of a small mistake in a dangerous situation can be fatal. It teaches us to be careful.

WATER

Like gravity, water is another essential aspect of earth. Without water, our planet could not support life. If all food and water disappeared today, we would die from dehydration first. But we have to be aware of the dangers of water, be it in a lake, flood, ocean, or bathtub. Of all the places that water can be, you don't want it filling your lungs. In 2014, there were 3,406 accidental drownings.[3] Water is always dangerous and requires our respect and an awareness of its risks.

FIRE

Whether we have a furnace that burns natural gas, a boiler that burns oil, or a stove that burns wood, we need fire to warm ourselves on cold days. We also require fire to cook our food. So fire plays an indispensable role in our survival. But as we all know, fire also must be respected and handled with care. In 2014, there were 2,701 deaths by fire[4] and untold thousands of burn injuries. Forest, range, home, and business fires cost millions of dollars of damage each year. As children, we learn about the dangers of fire and the fact that burns are the most painful injuries we can suffer. Fire also teaches us the value of respect and caution.

WIND

Wind is simply the movement of air from one location of high atmospheric pressure to other locations of lower atmospheric pressure. Wind is what pushes evaporated water from the ocean into the sky and over landmasses, where it can become rain for the earth. The drag of wind over vast areas of the oceans causes currents that stir up the ocean and spread nutrients to its far corners.[5] Windstorms lift vast quantities of dust from the drylands and then deposit it in the ocean (providing needed minerals to ocean plankton) or onto the rain forests (providing those same minerals to growing plants).[6] Wind moderates temperatures throughout the world, keeping the polar icecaps from getting too cold and the equatorial regions from getting too hot.

Yet, weather patterns can also generate dangerous, life-threatening winds. Under certain conditions, warm fronts mix with cold fronts to form whirlwinds over a low-pressure center. The revolving winds accelerate and, if conditions are just right, become tornadoes (over land) or hurricanes (over sea). Both endanger the lives of the people who live underneath these cyclones and do millions of dollars of damage each year. Mankind has gained the knowledge to monitor the weather and give warning when a hurricane or tornado is approaching. We have learned to build shelters that withstand high winds and ferocious storms. Cyclones are still a danger, but over the years, we have learned how to reduce their threat.

As explained in the opening pages of this book, God does not create hurricanes to afflict us. Natural forces of weather within our atmosphere cause them. For example, Earth is not the only planet with cyclones. The Red Spot of Jupiter is a large cyclone that continually moves across the surface of the planet. This hurricane is twice the size of Earth and has lasted for at least 350 years. God did not create that storm to afflict His children either.

Rain

Rain is, of course, essential to our lives. Rainfall refreshes our land, crops, and livestock. When we have no rain, drought causes crops to die and people to starve. The rain-making process is actually quite complex. Clouds are caused by water vapor rising from the earth. As it hits the colder temperatures of higher elevations, the vapor condenses into very small water droplets that stay suspended in the air. If there is a sufficient updraft, it will push these water droplets higher into the colder altitudes, where they collide and form even larger water drops. These drops grow so large that they cannot be suspended by the upward drafts any longer and start falling to earth. On their way down, these tiny raindrops merge with each and grow larger. Thus, while smaller clouds provide gentle summer showers, tall thunderheads can deliver storms that cause flooding, mud-slides, and erosion.[7]

With flooding comes danger—but it is a danger that can be managed with wisdom. In the spring after moving to Minnesota, I remember the news reporting that residents of the Red River Valley north of us were experiencing severe flooding. Numerous volunteers and youth groups, including my children, drove up to fill and place sand bags to protect homes and businesses. I felt terrible for the residents who lived there. Then, just two years later, the Red River flooded again. A year or two later, it flooded yet again. I then realized that the residents for whom I had felt such pity had built their homes in the Red River flood plain. Is this wisdom? We should note at this point that floods do have their upside. Floods bring needed nutrients and organic material to farmlands, naturally fertilizing the soil. The best example of this action can be found in the annual flooding of the Nile River, which has refreshed the delta farmlands of Egyptian kingdoms for over five thousand years. The ancient Egyptians wisely learned to work with the floods, not against them. For millennia, Egypt has not tried to restrict or control the flooding of the Nile, nor did they ever build their pyramids and houses on its flood plain.

Volcanoes

Every minute of every day, the earth is bombarded with a steady stream of high-energy particles, both from the sun and from outer space. These high-energy particles are similar to the particles emitted by a radioactive element such as uranium. Though of a lower intensity, being under a continuous shower of such radiation would cause us increased levels of cancer, DNA damage, birth defects, and other radiation sickness. Unprotected from such radiation, life on earth would certainly be different, if not impossible. Fortunately for us, the earth has a strong magnetic field that deflects most of these high-energy particles from hitting us. So, one might ask, "From where does that magnetic field come?"

The inner core of the earth is a solid ball of nickel-iron alloy. The outer core of the earth, extending from 1800 to 3200 miles beneath our feet, is mostly hot (5000 °C), semi-liquid iron called magma.[8] Due to both the earth's rotation and large temperature and density fluctuations, magma moves continuously around the nickel-iron inner core of our planet. The movement of this very conductive liquid metal sets up an electrical current in the magma—and that current causes a magnetic field so strong that it extends into space itself. This magnetic field deflects the cosmic high-energy particles so they go around the earth instead of through us. Incredibly, the magma under the earth keeps all of us alive on the surface of the earth.

But there is a downside to magma as well. Volcanoes are caused by the upsurgence of magma from the outer core of the earth. Magma can come up through a weak spot in the earth's crust (such as in Hawaii) or up through the fault lines where the earth's tectonic plates come together. So, most of the world's volcanoes occur along the seams of converging tectonic plates (subduction zones) or the seams of diverging plates (rift zones).[9] One of the most famous volcanoes in our earth's history is Mt.

Vesuvius in Southern Italy. Vesuvius has erupted over thirty times, but its most famous eruption took place in AD 79, when Vesuvius caused lava and ash to cover the nearby city of Pompeii. The exact death toll will never be known, but archeologists have discovered the remains of over one thousand ash-preserved victims. Apparently, those victims had no warning. Things are different today.

The most famous volcanic eruption in the modern United States occurred at Mount St. Helens, near Spokane, Washington. At 8:32 a.m. on May 18, 1980, an eruption occurred that blew away the mountain's north face and shot hot ash sixteen miles into the air. Fifty-seven people died, thousands of animals were killed, and two hundred square miles of forest were obliterated.

Yet . . . in defense of the volcano . . . earthquakes had been occurring in the Mount St. Helens' area for two months before the eruption. A large explosion on the summit created a new crater and blew ash over a large area of the mountain. A month before the eruption, the northern face of Mount St. Helens began to visibly swell. The eruption that finally occurred was no surprise, and the fifty-seven people who died in it were well aware that the danger of staying in the area had become critical.[10] We have developed the technology to predict volcanic eruptions. If we have the wisdom to heed the warnings given by that technology, volcanoes should be less dangerous.

EARTHQUAKES

When the earth was very young, it was also nearly featureless. In those days, all the earth was a molten mass of magma. Gravity pulled the viscous magma into the tightest packing it could, making the young earth a rather featureless sphere. As the magma on the surface cooled, it hardened into our earth's mantle. As water was formed by chemical reaction or gathered from icy meteorites, a continuous but shallow ocean covered the earth. Gradually, under pressures from the magma underneath, the mantle broke into pieces that we now call "tectonic plates."

Where the internal pressure was highest, magma continued to push up through the plate seams and put pressure on the two plates to move out of the way. Over millions of years, when two tectonic plates collided, one plate would be swept up on top of the other. As the plates collided and folded upon themselves, massive mountain ranges were formed. Deep valleys and canyons were also created and, once filled with run-off water, became our deep oceans and seas. So, tectonic plates had a major role in creating the beautiful—and dry—lands upon which we live.

The earth has about fifteen major tectonic plates on it now and a number of smaller plates as well. These plates are still in contact with each another but continue to move. Fault lines are where the plates contact each other. They are generally found along the coast where land meets ocean. These points of contact push against one another with the weight of entire continents. When one of these contact points crumble, the tectonic plate slips a bit. On the surface, we feel the jolt of that movement as an earthquake. As one might expect, minor earthquakes are caused by a few smaller rocks breaking. Major earthquakes are caused by breaks that cause more dramatic shifts of the tectonic plate under them. A major quake is often followed by aftershock tremors that occur as the new fault lines settle into place against each other.

Unlike volcanoes and floods, earthquakes are hard to predict. However, through their explorations and data collection, geologists have determined where the fault lines lie. Obviously, earthquakes are dangerous and destructive. To avoid the danger of earthquakes, the wisest strategy would be to not live over a fault line, but fault lines are right along coastal regions, and people like to live near the beach. The most famous fault line in the world is the San Andreas Fault, which is the contact point of two of the largest tectonic plates in the world. East of the fault lies the North American Plate, which supports the USA, Canada, Mexico, and half of the Atlantic Ocean. To the west of the fault line is the massive Pacific Plate, which supports most of the Pacific Ocean. While San Francisco sits on top of the North American Plate, the other major cities of California sit upon the Pacific Plate. The San Andreas Fault runs along the entire coast of California, with the Pacific Plate slipping north and the North American Plate sliding south. Each year, Southern California has about ten thousand earthquakes. Most of them are so small that they are not even felt. But several hundred register greater than 3.0 on the Richter scale, and about fifteen to twenty register higher than 4.0, which is the point when some property damage is expected to occur.[11]

I am not suggesting that the millions of Californians who live, work, and drive over the San Andreas Fault should all move out of the state, but when the next big earthquake does happen, people will undoubtedly question why God allowed such a disaster to happen. Well, there is no question as to why it happens. Californians have had many years to either prepare for major earthquakes or move away from them. Most Californians are pretty nonchalant about earthquakes. They have decided that the advantages of living in California outweigh the dangers. It is, of course, their right to choose, but when the next big earthquake hits—and we are assured by seismologists that it will—we should remember our choices and accept whatever consequences befall us because of them.

Tsunamis

When a strong undersea earthquake occurs beneath the ocean floor, it abruptly pushes up on one of the immense plates of the earth's crust. That sudden movement displaces an enormous amount of ocean water. From a satellite, the wave produced looks like the ripples on a pond caused by a thrown rock. These huge waves become a tsunami, spreading outward in every direction from the epicenter of an earthquake. In March 2011, a 9.1 magnitude earthquake occurred 231 miles northeast of Tokyo. The quake caused a tsunami with thirty-foot waves that crashed into the nearest coasts of Japan. Nearly twenty thousand lives were lost. It was learned later that surviving the tsunami depended heavily on whether effective evacuation orders were given and then followed. Warning sirens sounded for about forty-five minutes before the tsunami. Those who heeded recommended procedures were able to make it to safety in time. Many of those who did not understand the instructions, or thought they could grab precious objects from their home before fleeing, died.[12] Disasters often force decisions upon us that must be made immediately. Once again, mankind has developed technology to reduce the dangers of earth life—if those threatened have the wisdom to use it.

The Dangers of Plants and Animals

From the very beginning, both plants (Genesis 1:11) and animal species (Genesis 1:22, 24) were given the commandment by God to be fruitful and multiply. In order to do this, every species of plant and animal has to get enough to eat, protect itself from being eaten, mature, find a mate, and have offspring. Some species then have the added responsibility of feeding those offspring until they are old enough to survive on their own.

In His directive, God did *not* tell the plants and animals to leave mankind alone. They could afflict man and defend themselves against him as well.

For most of our time here, one of the challenges of earth life has been to deal with dangerous plants and animals. To their credit, plants and animals have evolved an astonishing array of capabilities to survive and multiply. Plants grew thorns, spines, and prickles to prevent humans or animals from eating them. Other plants developed poisons to discourage their consumption. Once matured, plants evolved to disperse their seeds in a number of ways. Some trees and plants cast their seeds to the wind attached to tufts of cotton, whirlybird wings, or tumbleweeds. Others have seeds with clinging hooks or spines to attach themselves to a passing animal. Fortunately for us, some trees and vegetables evolved that placed their seeds in the middle of delicious fruit. Birds, animals and humans eat the fruit and thereby the seeds. These mobile creatures transport the seeds to new ground and deposit the seeds there. Make no mistake. The apple tree in your garden is not growing fruit for your benefit. It is growing fruit hoping that its seeds will be planted elsewhere to carry on the lineage of that apple tree. As promised to Adam as he was leaving the Garden of Eden (Genesis 3:18), the earth now brings forth a large variety of thorns and thistles. These and other weeds have developed uncanny abilities to survive despite all the hoeing, plucking, and weed killers we throw at them. When the Lord commanded, "Be fruitful and multiply," the plants obeyed.

Animals have the same directive and command to survive and multiply. They too have to eat and avoid being eaten to achieve that goal. Birds have the ability to fly away from danger. Many land animals have the ability to flee quickly from danger. Other animals live most of their lives in trees, which is safer for them than the ground. Some animals have shear bulk and strength to resist attackers. Animals have evolved sharp teeth and claws, stingers, a poisonous bite, thick shells, or even electric shock to protect themselves from attack. The law of the jungle is real. The meat-eaters on earth must kill other animals to survive and feed their offspring. They too have developed speed, camouflage, and strength to better enable them to chase down and kill their prey. Carnivores live in all realms—the air, the ocean, rivers, and land. In earlier eons, man was routinely hunted by the meat-eaters of the planet. Today we keep many wild animals in zoos and wildlife parks where we can enjoy the thrill of being near them without the danger. Incredibly, many people still figure out ways to breach the barriers and expose themselves to danger. The folly of such actions indicates that we are forgetting much of the wisdom learned by our ancestors.

COULD A WORLD WITHOUT DANGER EXIST?

In each of the examples given, we can see that extremes are destructive. Gravity is not dangerous if you are dropping ten inches, but it will hurt you if dropping ten feet. Too little rain gives us drought. Too much rain causes floods. In either case, people often die.

It is mankind's task to learn to control the extremes of nature. In a large part, we have done that. We have learned to irrigate to avoid the famines caused by drought. We have learned to build levees and dikes to control flooding. Commercial buildings and homes are designed to better survive earthquakes. We have the technology to warn us of oncoming hurricanes, volcanoes, and even tsunamis. We have formed emergency response teams trained to fight fires and others to rescue citizens from disasters that we cannot divert.

But one has to wonder. Did gravity, water, fire, wind, rain, magma, and tectonic plates all have to come with dangers? Could we have had a planet with gravity that holds us to earth but cuts off if we fall? Is it possible to have water we can drink but not drown us? Could weather patterns have been programmed to provide only gentle summer rains without the dangers of thunderstorms, blizzards, and hailstorms? Could we have the protection that magma gives us from cosmic rays without having it occasionally erupt from our volcanoes, destroying life and property? Could our tectonic plates have given us our beautiful mountains, oceans, and landscapes without now threatening us with earthquakes?

I have no references and I have no proof, but I don't think such a child-proofed world exists. Our earth life is exceedingly beautiful, giving us a variety of sceneries, temperatures, weather, foods, plants, and animals, but sometimes the extremes of that diversity can be dangerous. These are both facts of life and rules of earth. Earth was designed to thrill us, stretch us, try us, and challenge us. Would we want to live on a world where there were no consequences to our actions? Could we have learned the wisdom of avoiding danger and caring for ourselves in a world where there were no dangers? I don't believe we would. It is hard to take danger seriously if it is only being described to you. We have to live with the dangers and learn from them, but God does not have to create dangers and natural disasters. They were programmed into earth life from the very start. As Rabbi Kushner summarized,

> Insurance companies refer to earthquakes, hurricanes, and other natural disasters as "acts of God." I consider that a case of using God's name in vain. I don't believe that an earthquake that kills thousands of innocent victims without reason is an act of God. It is an act of nature. Nature is morally blind. It churns along, following its own laws, not caring who or what gets in the way.[13]

I agree with Rabbi Kushner, but I also think the earth was made with the purpose of teaching us wisdom, humility, and a healthy respect for nature. If nature was designed to "churn along, following its own laws . . ." then it is our responsibility to learn wisdom to stay out of its way.

Chapter 7

Learning as a World

Learning wisdom must be very important to our moral education, because the cost of that learning has been immense. Most earthly dangers exist to teach us as individuals. As just reviewed, gravity, fire, prickly pear cactus, and skunks teach us each personal wisdom. Each delivers an immediate consequence to a bad decision on our part. But some challenges to our well-being cannot be overcome by our wisdom alone. These dangers are so severe and complicated that it takes all of mankind to address them.

Disease is the best example of an earthly challenge that we had to solve as the human race. The war against bacteria and viruses has been brutal. No other earthly danger has killed more of our fellow humans. Casualties number in the millions. Diseases have been such a dire threat to humanity that they required thousands of doctors and hundreds of years to overcome. Communicable disease is a unique earthly challenge. To reduce the danger of being attacked by a lion, I just have to be alert and stay away from lions, but the millions of people who have died from disease did nothing wrong or unwise. The only bad decision they made was to be around someone who was sick, and they almost certainly had no idea they risked contamination as they did.

As an entire people, we had to discover how to fight disease. Throughout history, doctors had to learn from each disease outbreak, share what they learned with each other, and try to develop potential cures. Against this foe, wisdom had to be gathered in a long-term, worldwide effort.

Viruses, Bacteria, and Plagues

Though viruses and bacteria have killed millions of people over thousands of years, they are microscopic and fragile organisms. Most bacteria must live in water with very moderate temperature, acidity, and salinity. By our definition of life, viruses are not even *living*. They are so small that they can barely be distinguished by an electron microscope and they must reside in the cells of another organism to survive. But both viruses and bacteria still have the mandate to be fruitful and multiply. They do this by invading, multiplying, and spreading throughout a host organism. Once established and multiplying, bacteria and viruses invade the body fluids of the host—saliva, stomach contents, urine, and feces. When those bodily fluids are expelled, the bacteria or virus can spread to those good-hearted souls who clean up the mess. Coughing, a very common symptom of infections, sprays germ-laden saliva into the air. When they are inhaled into the warm, moist, hospitable environment of the lungs of a new host, the germs have a new fertile field for reproduction. The infection spreads. Despite all appearances, the bacteria or virus that is killing its human host is not evil. It does not have a brain or a murderous intent. It is just following the Lord's command to be fruitful and multiply.

From the comfort and stability of our modern-day lives, it is nearly impossible to truly understand the devastation wrought by plagues. But to illustrate the importance of this rule of earth, we need to review a few of the worst plagues that afflicted man over the centuries. This history is saddening. Yet, in the midst of our own trials, history can give us some perspective on how bad circumstances have been for other peoples. Only catastrophes of this magnitude can give us insight into the importance God has placed on us gathering our own knowledge and developing cures for disease. If He was ever going to set aside a rule of earth, it would have been during the worst plagues, but He didn't do that. No task in the history of mankind has been more difficult than learning to defeat bacteria and viruses.

The First Recorded Plagues

Plagues have existed for many centuries, but we are only aware of those that were documented by the historians of the time. As the population of men grew and came together in larger cities, with merchants, soldiers, and others traveling between those population centers, contagious diseases had more numerous opportunities to spread further and faster. For example, in the fifth century BC, Greece was a world power and Athens was its large and busy capital. In 430 BC, a plague hit Athens that killed about half of the population.[1, 2] Symptoms were described as "a very rapid onset, raging fever, extreme thirst, tongue and throat "bloody," the skin of the body red and livid, finally breaking into pustules and ulcers."[3] We are still unsure what the disease actually was. It could have been the first appearance of scarlet fever or bubonic plague in Europe. A new disease would explain the high death toll, since no immunity would have had time to develop.

In the first and second centuries AD, the Roman Empire was at the height of its power. Its holdings spread from Great Britain along both shores of the Mediterranean Ocean to the Middle East. The Romans had brought needed order and civilization to many of these areas. Rome was the epicenter of the empire and, as the saying goes, "All roads led to Rome." That fact was its undoing. In AD 160, one man, probably a soldier returning home from Mesopotamia, brought an enemy to Rome that its vast and well-trained armies could not combat—the variola or smallpox virus. The result was called the Antonine plague. This plague caused fever blisters and rash to suddenly break out over the entire body. Victims would develop fevers, inflammation of the tongue and throat, diarrhea, and extreme thirst. From these descriptions of its symptoms, the sickness was probably smallpox. This particular plague lasted for over thirty years.

In AD 250, Rome was again attacked by a major plague. This one was called the plague of Cyprian. A Catholic bishop of Carthage, Cyprian was the historian who documented this plague. He described symptoms as being violent diarrhea, vomiting, fever, and gangrene of the hands and feet. The doctors of the time were completely baffled, and it would take over a thousand years to develop a cure. The identity of the plague of Cyprian is still uncertain, but it lasted for sixteen years and spread to all corners of the Roman Empire. Mortality was reported to have been over 50 percent is some areas.[4]

Bubonic Plague—aka the Black Death

In the 1330s, a particularly virulent strain of bubonic plague broke out in China and Mongolia. It went on to become the most-traveled plague of its time. From China, the virus was carried by unknowing but infected travelers to Crimea on the north shores of the Black Sea. Following established trade routes, the disease headed both west into Europe and south into the Middle East. The disease spread to Italy in 1348 and then to France, Germany, Scandinavia, and the rest of Europe. By the time it was over, the disease had struck virtually every corner of the civilized world.

We know now that the responsible bacteria, Pasteurella pestis, now referred to as Yersinia pestis, was first passed to man from infected black rats. Fleas would bite an infected rat, transfer to a human host, and then bite them, passing along the bacteria. The first symptom of bubonic plague was the emergence of bumps or "bubos" in the groin, neck, or armpits, caused by the swelling of the lymphatic glands there. Due to the black spots that appeared on the skin and the fact that death usually occurred within three days, the disease earned its nickname "The Black Death." While this original form of the disease caused more than a few deaths, you could protect yourself from it by simply staying away from rats and fleas. So the Black Death would have probably been a minor disease if it had continued to use fleas as its only vector. However, the Pasteurella pestis bacteria evolved and "learned" to infect human lungs instead of our lymphatic system. The respiratory form of the disease could now be passed to whole groups of people through the cough of just one infected person. Transmission rates increased and death rates soared.

Over the centuries of battling this disease, multiple theories sprang up as to the medical reasons for the Black Death. The miasma theory was popular and proposed that bad air and putrid smells caused the disease. Thus the afflicted would put flowers or onions throughout the house to purify the air. One cure involved eating crushed emeralds. Other theories involved putting frogs, pigeons, onions, and figs on the bubos to draw out the poison. Bloodletting was an ineffective treatment used for many years.[5]

It is estimated that about thirty-seven million people died in Asia from the Black Death.[6] In Europe, about twenty-four million people, or about one quarter of its population, died of the same plague.[7] Authors of the time frankly stated that future generations would never appreciate the effects of this plague across the entire Eurasian continent. I agree with them. We cannot imagine the emptied villages, churches filled with dead bodies, and utter silence in what should have been bustling towns and roads. Physicians were helpless, having had no idea what was causing the deaths of their patients. Priests and church leaders had no answers either.

A man named Agnolo di Tura of Siena, Italy, wrote the following description:

> Father abandoned child, wife, husband; one brother, another, for this illness seemed to strike through the breath and the sight. And so they died. And no one could be found to bury the dead for money or for friendship . . . And in many places in Siena great pits were dug and piled deep with huge heaps of the dead.[8]

There are two historical aspects of the bubonic plague that should be noted for consideration in modern times. In both circumstances, faithful Christians believed that the plague was a curse sent by God—and some thought they knew how to avoid it. The first group with this mistaken conclusion was called the Brotherhood of the Flagellants. As the name might suggest, the Flagellants performed acts of self-flagellation in penance for their sins. In groups of several hundred, the brethren would march into a city, gather the townspeople, and perform their scourging. These lashings, performed three times a day, were often severe enough to draw blood. During their month-long pilgrimages, flagellants could not bathe or change clothes. Their belief was that God would recognize their painful, public penance as punishment enough for their sins and keep the Black Plague from afflicting them. You may laugh at the concept today, but you may know someone who has done their own penance—not because they had sinned and needed to repent, but because random disaster has struck them. Like the Brotherhood of Flagellants, they reason that the disaster must be divine retribution for something, so they must scourge themselves. Such self-inflicted punishment assumes that God could avert the results of the tragedy if He was motivated enough by your penance. In reality, that logic didn't make sense in 1348 and it doesn't make any sense today.

The second approach Europe took to alleviate the plague was to blame the Jews. The Jewish people had already endured much persecution and would suffer more in their future. Throughout history, Christians justified their non-Christian abuse of Jews by pointing out that it was the Jewish people, after all, who crucified the Savior. They reasoned that the

Jews must be under God's condemnation so they deserved whatever persecutions they received. During the years of the Black Death, this persecution intensified. Perhaps in order to justify the violence, a rumor was started that Jews were purposefully contaminating water wells with the plague. The fact that their Jewish neighbors were dying at the same rate as Christians did not seem to squelch the rumor or dissuade the persecutors. Thousands of Jews were hanged, burned, or forcibly evicted from their homes, mostly in France, Switzerland, and Western Germany. Good Christians (or, in this case, not so good) concluded that Jews were the cause of their afflictions and they needed to kill or banish them, though such hostility went against all of the teachings of Christ Himself.

These are two examples of the evil that can be wrought by believers *who think they know the causes of disaster and how to turn away God's wrath.* Obviously, these persecutors did *not* know the cause of the plagues. Their assumption that the sins of the people caused the plagues was wrong and simply added to the pain and misery of the time. The plagues were a hazard of earth life, not a punishment from God. From our viewpoint of looking back upon history, it is easy for us to see that now. We need to take that understanding and apply it to disasters for which we blame others today.

Plagues in the New World

We know that tens of millions of people died in Europe and Asia in the centuries before the development of vaccines and medicines. The illnesses, symptoms, and death tolls were often fairly well documented. We have less information about the plagues that afflicted the New World, but we do know that European explorers and conquerors brought some of the worst plagues seen in the Americas. As Jared Diamond explains in *Guns, Germs and Steel*,

> The importance of lethal microbes in human history is well illustrated by Europeans' conquest and depopulation of the New World. Far more Native Americans died in bed from Eurasian germs than on the battlefield from European guns and swords. These germs undermined Indian resistance by killing most Indians and their leaders and by sapping the survivors' morale.[9]

The Demise of the Aztec Empire

In 1519, Hernán Cortés landed on the coasts of Mexico with a small force of six hundred Spaniards. When he and his men reached the Aztec capital of Tenochtitlan, the native people greeted them warmly. But Cortés had a goal to conquer Mexico and take its gold. When he imprisoned the emperor Montezuma and held him for ransom, relations soured. In June 1520, Cortés was driven out of Tenochtitlan, losing most of his army in the process. However, unwittingly, the Spaniards had left behind an infection of smallpox. By September the Aztecs, "were covered with agonizing sores from head to foot . . . the sick were so utterly helpless they could only lie on their beds like corpses, unable to move their limbs or even their heads."[10] When Cortés returned with a reinforced army a few years later, there was little resistance to his invasion. The Aztec Empire was defeated, and Mexico became a colony of Spain for the next three hundred years. In total, it is estimated that smallpox killed about eighteen million of the twenty million people of Mexico over the course of a few years.[11]

The Demise of the Incan Empire

In 1500, the Incan Empire encompassed most of the western half of South America. This empire had developed irrigated food production, active trade, and a rich culture. The advancements and infrastructure of the Incas were impressive, as visitors to Machu Picchu are taught in their tours. It is believed that around 1525, a single infected Spaniard introduced the smallpox virus into the Empire. Within two years, the Incan emperor Huayna Capac, his successor, numerous political leaders, and army generals had died of the disease. Chaos reigned as civil war added to the death tolls. When Francisco Pizarro invaded in 1532, he had an army of only 168 men, but the smallpox virus had decimated the Incan population and its armies to the point that Pizzaro was able to defeat the new emperor Atahualpa and ransom him for a roomful of gold.[12] More Spaniard atrocities were to follow. The vast Incan empire, with thousands of warriors, was conquered by an enemy of one deadly virus and less than two hundred Spanish soldiers.

The Demise of Other Native American Peoples

Besides the Incas and Aztecs, there were many other populations of Native Americans. Due to its rich land and inexhaustible water supply, many of these natives lived in the Mississippi Valley. No Spanish conquistadors ever attacked or overthrew this region of the Americas. These were mostly agrarian-based tribes with no gold or silver to be taken. Yet as Europeans continued to arrive at the shores of the new American continents, contact between the native populations and sick immigrants was inevitable. Newly infected natives traveled home and exposed everyone in their villages to the plague they unknowingly carried.

European diseases eventually traveled throughout the entire Western Hemisphere. In 1540, Hernando de Soto became the first European explorer to visit the Central United States. In his travels, he found Native American villages emptied by plague and survivor abandonment. The population of the island of Hispaniola was totally wiped out. After Captain Cook and other European explorers visited Hawaii, a series of diseases reduced its population by nearly half a million. We will never know the total body count in the Americas due to smallpox, measles, influenza, typhus, diphtheria, malaria, mumps, bubonic plague, tuberculosis, and yellow fever. It was one of the most difficult times in Earth's history. Bacteria and viruses killed millions of innocents, while men on another continent learned how to prevent and cure those diseases.

Why Me?

I don't want to minimize the pain and trials of modern-day Christians, but when I hear someone who is struggling with a divorce, job loss, or financial challenge ask, "Why did God allow this to happen to me?" I think about the struggles of our ancestors and the wholesale deaths they faced before the advent of modern medicine. As they lost friends and families to plagues and suffered severe physical torments of their own, do you think our ancestors ever thought, "Why is this happening to me? What did I do to deserve this punishment?" The answer is certainly, "Yes, they did." It seems to be a human trait to turn to God for answers to the "Why me?" questions of life. Europeans, Asians, and Native Americans all turned to their gods in the face of the sweeping epidemics that caused wholesale death and despair. We know this, because many of these plague victims died in their places of worship. After the "Why me?" in their prayers, inevitably these afflicted innocents must have asked God, "Can you please make it stop?" They just wanted an end to the nightmare that had started with the simple contact of one culture with another.

Looking back with the knowledge we have of the causes of disease and the death tolls they caused, let us consider the answers to these questions. Of the millions of people who died from the plagues of the Middle Ages, how many of them do you think were being punished for their individual sins? Were any of them supposed to learn something from their loss and suffering? Please remember, these plagues occurred in the middle of the Great Apostasy and Dark Ages. Europeans knew of Jesus Christ, but the restoration of the gospel was centuries away. The Native Americans of the time certainly did not know anything about Jesus Christ, repentance, or the gospel. So what were they supposed to learn from their trials that make ours pale by comparison? Does anyone really believe that God engineered the pain-wracked deaths of millions of people as retribution for a sin or to teach them something? Of course He did not. God did not send the plagues, but He knew they were coming, and He had to allow them to happen.

Just like a child must go to school to learn how to survive adulthood, mankind had to learn how to survive earth life. The knowledge to practice basic sanitation, immunize ourselves from viruses, and treat bacterial infections with antibiotics had to be learned. God could not just hand us this wisdom. Obviously, such free knowledge would also have violated the requirement that the earth remain a place of faith. At a huge cost, mankind determined that there is a dangerous microbiological element on this earth that must be controlled. The knowledge was hard-won by the efforts of thousands of scientists—most of them unrenowned for their efforts. If fame was proportional to their contributions to the good of mankind, then Edward Jenner, Joseph Lister, Louis Pasteur, Alexander Fleming, and other medical practitioners like them would be internationally acclaimed heroes.

LATEST PLAGUES

Until recently, influenza was the last major epidemic in the United States—first striking almost a hundred years ago. The disease appeared in the United States in March 1918 in Fort Riley, Kansas. In October, twenty-one thousand U.S. deaths were recorded in one week, the highest weekly mortality in our history.[13] World War I facilitated the transport of the disease to all parts of the world since soldiers were crowded together in army camps and then sent to the battle front in Europe to fight the Germans. Influenza does not take sides in a war. It is reported that 228,000 Britons died of the disease, as did 225,000 Germans.[14] In the U.S., 548,000 died; worldwide, the disease is blamed for 21,000,000 deaths.[15] Our latest disease scare was from an Ebola outbreak in Africa in 2014. About 11,325 people died, two of which died in the United States.[16]

CORONAVIRUS

As I write these words, the world is dealing with a new coronavirus disease called COVID-19 that has just been ruled a pandemic by the World Health Organization. To slow the spread of COVID-19, church services, sporting events, theaters, and other events that bring people together have been shut down. Schools and universities have closed across the country. We are seeing long lines in grocery stores as people prepare for the worst. As of today, over seven thousand people have died from the virus, and the lives of millions of people have been turned upside down. Few people have ever seen anything like this, and many are fearful.

As individuals, we are often given severe trials to make us stronger and more resilient. Occasionally, one particular society or country will have a significant challenge they must overcome. Only rarely does the whole world receive a threat to which it must respond immediately and decisively. But, so far, earth governments are responding. Petty differences are being set aside, and world leaders are cooperating to reduce the death toll of this disease. COVID-19 will be a harsh and expensive reminder that, even in the year 2020, the earth is a dangerous place. We as a people must again rise to this challenge as we have throughout our history. As we fight this latest common enemy, the human race will be stronger and more knowledgeable for it efforts. Hopefully, too, each one of us can learn wisdom, fortitude, and strength as we deal with this latest adversity.

THE AGE OF IGNORANCE AND GENETIC DISORDERS

From 430 BC through AD 1800, doctors throughout the world meticulously observed and documented the symptoms of epidemics, but in all this time, they could not determine the causes of the diseases or how to treat them. It's not that they didn't try. Multiple treatments, many of which appear ridiculous today, were proposed and attempted without success. Centuries passed. In the end, it took over two thousand years before researchers discovered the specific bacteria and viruses that were the source of plagues. Antimicrobials and vaccines were developed, and the diseases were pushed back. Since then, we have witnessed so many advances in the field of medicine that it is easy to believe that mankind's age of ignorance is behind us. But it is not. While most bacterial and viral diseases of the body have been identified and cured, most ailments due to genetic flaws remain unresolved.

AUTISM

Autism was once considered a rare disorder. In the early 1980s, it was estimated that autism affected about one out of every 2200 births. Then diagnoses started to increase. At first, the increases were chalked up to a greater awareness (and thus diagnosis) of the disorder. Most assuredly, this explained part of the rise, but not all of it. In 2000, the Center for Disease Control (CDC) started recording the prevalence of autism among eight-year-olds, when the occurrence was one out of 150 children. By 2014, the prevalence of autism spectrum disorder had increased to one in 59 children.[17]

Autism is officially called Autism Spectrum Disorder (ASD), because not everyone who has autism behaves in the same way. Development problems are spread across many areas of learning and communication. ASD commonly afflicts those with other developmental, psychiatric, neurologic, chromosomal, or genetic problems as well. All of this makes accurate diagnosis difficult, which is only the first of many frustrations for parents of autistic children. As the CDC admits,

> Diagnosing ASD can be difficult since there is no medical test, like a blood test, to diagnose the disorders. Doctors look at the child's behavior and development to make a diagnosis.[18]

Like early doctors cast about for the causes and remedies to influenza and smallpox, doctors and parents today are proposing myriads of causes and treatments for autism. Environmental toxins have been blamed. The mercury-based preservative once added to vaccines was blamed for a while. When pharmaceutical providers discontinued using the preservative, no change was seen in the number of new ASD prognoses. So, with that theory proven wrong, the blame shifted to the vaccines themselves. This myth has shown amazing resiliency over the years. In 1998, a physician named Andrew Wakefield published a paper suggesting that the vaccine for measles, mumps, and Rubella (MMR) caused autism. It turned out Wakefield was a fraud who had fabricated his data. The paper was retracted, and Wakefield was stripped of his medical license, but the myth continued to be propagated. To convince anxious parents, multiple studies have been run to determine if vaccines could affect the brain and trigger autism. Each study has failed to find any such causation. Unfortunately, many frantic families and a few people craving media attention have ignored these definitive results. Out of love for their young children, numerous misguided parents are not having their young children vaccinated, a mistake which introduces an entirely new set of problems and concerns into the world.

Causes of autism may include genetic predisposition, the age of either parent at conception, drugs taken during pregnancy, low birth weight, or random environmental issues. How these factors interrelate to finally express as the disease is unknown. For some unknown reason, boys are four times more likely to develop ASD than girls.[19] In any case, the treatments for autism are limited to helping manage symptoms. There is no cure. Again, the CDC recognizes this failure, but offer some hope.

> There are no medications that can cure ASD or treat the core symptoms. However, there are medications that can help some people with ASD function better. For example, medication might help manage high energy levels, inability to focus, depression, or seizures.[20]

ATTENTION DEFICIT DISORDER

Autism is not the only childhood disorder that is growing.

> Attention-deficit hyperactivity disorder (ADHD) is one of the most common reasons children are referred for mental health services. It affects as many as one in every 20 children. Although boys are three to four times more likely than girls to experience ADHD, the disorder affects both boys and girls. There are three main types of ADHD. One type is characterized by inattentiveness, one type is characterized by hyperactive or impulsive behavior, and the third type is combined—when children exhibit signs of both types.[21]

Like autism, ADHD is on the rise. In 2016, an estimated 5.4 million U.S. children from two to seventeen years of age (8.4 percent) had an ADHD disorder. About 62 percent of these children are taking medication.[22]

The causes of ADHD are still being researched, but genetics apparently plays a major role. About 30 to 40 percent of children diagnosed with ADHD have relatives with the same disorder. Brain scans reveal that the brains of children with ADHD differ from those of children without the disorder. Like autism, children and adolescents with ADHD are more likely to suffer from other disorders as well. About one-half of youth with ADHD have oppositional defiant disorder, one-quarter have an anxiety disorder, one-third have depression, and one-fifth suffer from a bipolar disorder.[23] Such disorder overlaps must be related, but they make both diagnosis and treatment especially difficult.

Like autism, there is no cure for ADHD, and parents can only manage the symptoms. The most common treatment for ADHD is a drug called methylphenidate, better known by its trade name Ritalin. Ritalin is a stimulant that is regulated as a controlled substance by the DEA but has shown improvements in children with ADHD.

Just like the fight against epidemics lasted for centuries, our doctors today are working to understand the cause of the increase in behavioral disorders. The brain is the most complicated organ in the human body, and we still don't understand much about it. However, there was a time when there was no cure for smallpox, yet the vaccine to treat smallpox was eventually developed. There was a time when we had no treatment for AIDS, but medications were eventually produced. Today, we have no medications to eradicate autism or ADHD, but we have learned from history that mankind can figure this health challenge out as well. We have our best people working on it.

In the meantime, for parents who are raising a child with some type of autism, ADD, or other disorder, please know that God did not send you this challenge. Your child and you have been burdened with a difficult, unexpected challenge. Similar medical mysteries have occurred throughout earth's history. Diseases that the families of your ancestors did not understand or know how to treat afflicted them also. Like them, the difficulties you face today are not your fault, your child's fault, or God's fault. The cause of autism has been shown to be linked to genetics, which will be discussed in the next chapter. Though progress has been made in the science, there is still obviously much that has not been discovered.

Chapter 8

Rule 4: You Must Play the Hand You Are Dealt

VOLTAIRE WAS A WELL-KNOWN PHILOSOPHER who was born in France in 1694. Besides writing deep philosophical essays, it is believed that he created the following advice for card players and everyone else born on earth. Voltaire really should have begun his quote with, "Life is like a card game."

> Each player must accept the cards life deals him or her: But once they are in hand, he or she alone must decide how to play the cards in order to win the game.

Gamblers routinely try to figure out how to be lucky at cards, but the mystery of how to be lucky at birth has been a question for thousands of years. Why is one spirit born to be a prince and another a pauper? Not remembering what happened in the premortal existence, we don't know if we had any choice as to where, when, or to whom we were born. Did we have a voice in the selection of our parents, or at least their financial wealth? Could we have refused to be born in the sixteenth century or into a third-world country?

One theory discussed in religious circles is that we were born into favorable circumstances in this world according to the level of our obedience and accomplishments in the premortal existence. After all, we believe that our afterlife will be determined by our obedience and righteousness on earth. So it seems logical to conclude that our place on earth was somewhat determined by our behavior in the premortal existence. We know that Jesus Christ was the greatest success story in the premortal existence, so much so that He became the Savior of all mankind. We know that Lucifer was the greatest disappointment in the premortal existence, rebelling against the plan of salvation to become Satan. Many Christians figure that their choices in the premortal existence fell somewhere between those two extremes and that their birth circumstances may reflect their level of faithfulness.

But the idea that our lives in the premortal existence carry over into earth life can be overdone. In the 1970s, an LDS-based musical called *Saturday's Warrior* became a popular stage and screenplay. The story opens in the premortal existence. According to the premise of the musical, while in the premortal existence, each of us knows the spirits of those who will become our family. We can initiate romances there that will eventually lead to our marriage on earth. Though the idea of finding our "soulmate" has been discouraged,[1] many people, especially newlyweds, still believe in it. While the play was a delightful story with some great music, we should realize its premise is purely fictional. For the time being, the reasons for our birth family, birthdate, and birthplace will remain behind the veil of forgetfulness.

BORN INTO POVERTY

For much of the history of the world, the stratification of social classes due to wealth and bloodlines made it nearly impossible for someone to move up the social ladder. If you were born poor, you were likely to remain poor for the rest of your life. This situation still exists for most of the world. If you are born into a third-world country, it is difficult to improve your lot in life. For hundreds of years, immigrating to the United States has been the dream of millions of people—simply because it gave them a real opportunity to better their lives.

But if we are born into humble circumstances, we should remember that the world was not created for us to achieve financial success. Nowhere in the scriptures will we find encouragement to become rich. In fact, it appears that God worries about us if we acquire wealth. As He a watched a rich, potential disciple walk away from dedicating himself fully to the Lord, Jesus declared, "It is easier for a camel to go through a needle's eye, than for a rich man to enter into the kingdom of God" (Luke 18:25). While "easier for a camel to go through a needle's eye" was an expression of the day that somewhat exaggerated the unlikelihood of an event, the Savior had made His point.

Scriptural evidence verifies that being rich can get in the way of the true purpose of life. During their mission to the Zoramites, Alma and Amulek observe a rather novel form of worship that took place on a tower called the Rameumptom. Only wealthy worshippers were allowed to climb onto the tower and pray. The rote prayer offered by everyone first confirmed that their (false) doctrines were true and then thanked God they were a chosen, special, and holy people. Obviously, these proud Zoramites bought into the faulty philosophy that those who are wealthy are the most favored of God. Alma quickly recognized that these worshippers' "hearts were set upon gold, and upon silver, and upon all manner of fine goods." It was such a depressing display that Alma spends the next five verses ranting about it to the Lord (Alma 31:26–30) before finally asking for blessings for himself and his companions.

A few days later, a large group of the financially poor Zoramites approached Alma and told him of their plight. Because of their poverty, they were not allowed to enter the synagogues or ascend the tower of Rameumptom to worship. What were they to do? Alma replies as follows:

> I say unto you, it is well that ye are cast out of your synagogues, that ye may be humble, and that ye may learn *wisdom*; for it is necessary that ye should learn *wisdom*; for it is because that ye are cast out, that ye are despised of your brethren because of your exceeding poverty, that ye are brought to a lowliness of heart; for ye are necessarily brought to be humble. And now, because ye are compelled to be humble blessed are ye; for a man sometimes, if he is compelled to be humble, seeketh repentance; and now surely, whosoever repenteth shall find mercy; and he that findeth mercy and endureth to the end the same shall be saved. (Alma 32:12–13; italics added)

Given the premise of this book, please note the two uses of the word "wisdom" in this scripture. Alma points out that it is actually a good thing they were cast out of their synagogues and despised by their richer brethren *because it taught them to be humble.* Humility encourages a person to repent, find mercy, and endure to the end. If the first goal of earth life is to gather wisdom, this group of poor Zoramites had just found some. If the second goal of earth life is to choose righteousness and worship God, poverty does not impede that choice. In fact, Alma concedes, poverty may help you make the correct choice.

The first point of this chapter is that you have to "play the cards you are dealt" at birth. If you are given a life of relative poverty, you will have to work harder to provide shelter and food for your family *as well as* gain knowledge and serve God. Millions of people have accomplished this feat, accepting the cards they were dealt and playing those cards the best they could. You will not be judged by the poor circumstances of your birth. You will be judged on how you live the life you are given.

BORN INTO DISABILITY

For centuries, people believed that God granted beauty to the fair, strength to the strong, and superior brains to the intelligent. Today we know that God did not personally provide you your looks, physical strength, or mental abilities at birth. Instead, at conception, you were dealt 20,000 genes on twenty-three chromosomes. These genes make up what is called your "genotype." When your genes produced proteins and used them to construct your body and brain, they created your infant "phenotype" or outward appearance. Your genotype continues to restore and add to your phenotype every day of your life.

Genes are amazing molecules in that they allow you to inherit characteristics from your parents yet still have the flexibility to add uniqueness to the person you are. Whether you have your father's intellect or your mother's good looks, it is because you inherited most all of your genotype from your parents. Probability dictates that you will also be similar in looks and personality to your siblings, since they started out with the same parental gene choices as you. But the choices were different. Each gene in your genotype was taken from your mother or your father. Unless you are an identical twin, the 20,000 gene choices made in constructing you were different from those of your siblings. Thus, one child will take after dad, and another will look like mom. Many siblings often look a lot alike—which usually helps them feel interconnected.

Genes were also designed to be flexible. The molecules that make up your genes are called "nucleotides," and you have about three billion pairs of them.[2] When you were conceived, each of these nucleotides had to be copied from either your mother's or father's DNA to form your final genotype. The copy process is almost flawless, but not quite. For every 100 million base pairs copied correctly, one is not. Thus, each of us has about sixty mutations in our genetic code that were not programmed to be there. Surprisingly, these transcribing errors actually seem to have a purpose. Francis Collins states,

> Most of those mutations occur in parts of the genome that are not essential, and therefore they have little or no consequence. The ones that fall in the more vulnerable parts of the genome are generally harmful, and are thus rapidly culled out of the population because they reduce reproductive fitness. But on rare occasions, a mutation will arise by chance that offers a slight degree of selective advantage.[3]

This selective advantage may be that the child has a little more resistance to a virus that has recently become an epidemic. Or the advantage may be that the child has a little more body fat that will help it survive the rigors of an ice age.[4] In either case, these genetic mutations will have brought more diversity into the human race to allow it to better adapt to changing physical conditions on earth. Whether the organism is a bacterium, plant, animal, or human, genetic variance seems to be designed to help a species survive changes in weather, available foods, or disease that could otherwise lead to its extinction. Because the mutated organism has a genetic advantage, it is more likely to reproduce. This slight advantage, building over the centuries, can swing an entire population to possess the improved gene, and it becomes the norm instead of the exception.

To fully understand genetics and its functionality, one has to accept the concept of evolution. Whether you fully accept evolution or not, you will still learn in any natural history museum that millions of species have gone extinct in earth's history because they did not have enough variance in their genetics to survive one of earth's changes. If we never want to go the way of the dinosaur, we should be thankful we have had the needed adaptations to continue as a species.

The Bad News of Genetic Variation

A repeated theme of this book has been that many of the blessings of earth come with their dangers. Genetic variance also has its significant downside. As stated above, mutations that strengthen the species are rare. It is much more common for the mutation to cause a genetic disorder, resulting in a baby born with disabilities.

Over six thousand genetic disorders have been identified in humans.[5] Many of these conditions are caused by one gene (out of the twenty thousand) that has been mutated. These so-called Mendelian disorders include Huntington's disease, cystic fibrosis, and hemophilia. More severe disorders occur when there is a problem with an entire chromosome. For example, if the chromosomes of the father or mother fail to divide correctly, the fetus can end up with either fewer or more than the twenty-three chromosomes it should have. Often such a severe genetic disruption results in an early miscarriage. As expressed by one medical text,

> Experts believe that up to 60% of spontaneous abortions at less than 90 days' gestation result from an abnormal number of fetal chromosome; offspring with some chromosomal abnormalities are probably never even implanted.[6]

Down syndrome is caused by the presence of an extra chromosome, but faulty chromosomal divisions can also result in the loss of genetic material or its translocation to another chromosome. Each stumble in the extraordinarily complex genetic construction of a human has its own detrimental effects on the resulting child. Finally, some genetic abnormalities and birth defects are caused by the interaction of at least two inherited abnormal genes. Neural tube defects, cleft lip, cleft palate, and certain diabetes are examples of these multifactorial disorders.

For most of us, our DNA includes genes that may be a little disappointing. Many people would like to be better looking, more talented in music or sports, maybe a little taller, and certainly have a better memory for names. For those born with genetic disorders, life presents much more serious challenges than forgetting a few names. The imperfect gene-copying process brings with it both flexibility that helps the species and disorders that afflict individuals. Just as we have the responsibility to help those born into poverty, we have the responsibility to assist those born into disability.

Smaller Genetic Variations Also Cause Difficulties

It is usually easy to see the consequences of major genetic disorders on a person's physical and mental abilities. Each genetic abnormality has identifiable characteristics associated with it. But certain very slight differences in DNA can also be recognized. For example, your chromosomes will give you a distinctive facial structure. Yes, everyone has two eyes, a nose, and a mouth, but each face is a little different from that of everyone else, and your brain is attuned to recognize those differences. Among thousands of people, you could still quite easily pick out your family and friends.

Knowing there is such variation in faces, it should not surprise us that there is at least an equal amount of variation in our brains. Personalities vary as much as faces do. We know that much of our personality is passed down to us by our parents. You may be outgoing and kind like your mother, serene and soft-spoken like your father, or some combination of both. Intelligence is also based on the DNA with which we are born. So, it should not be surprising that other aspects of your personality are also programmed by your genes.[7]

Some people are naturally obedient as children and remain active in the Church all their lives. Others will start faithful and then experience a radical personality change as they become adults. Some people have a natural rebellious streak that causes them to resist rules and authority even as children. Others have strong propensities to seek pleasure from alcohol and drugs.

Many Christians believe that within our bodies we have a spirit. This spirit is a child of our Heavenly Father, which is the reason we can call God our Heavenly Father. Our spirit communicates with the Holy Ghost, and He tries to communicate and persuade our mind as well. In almost every church meeting, we are encouraged to listen to the Holy Ghost and our own spirit. We are taught that we can either be carnally minded and not be influenced by your spirit or the Holy Ghost, or we can be spiritually minded and accept the promptings of both (2 Nephi 9:39; D&C 67:10).

As we deal with our sometimes difficult children, we should realize that some spirits have a greater challenge in influencing the brains of their bodies. Due to their genetics, some minds are just more resistant to spiritual promptings than others. This trait can be frustrating for parents, their child, and other family members. Some people might imply that if your son's spirit was stronger, he wouldn't be exhibiting this rebelliousness. But it appears that, like the Holy Ghost, the spirit within you can only prompt and subtly encourage you to obey the commandments. Your mind makes the final decisions.

Though genetics plays a large role in our decisions, we are also a product of our experiences. As we have experiences and learn from them, we can change our genetically based inclinations—for good or for bad. A rebellious person may eventually find that rebellion never allows one to find contentment and peace, which can be found in church worship. On the other hand, a kind person who has been cheated and taken advantage of will eventually learn to stop being kind. So there is hope for any child. The best thing parents of a wayward child can do is to provide the most positive environment possible for their family (home, church, and school) and then pray for their children to find good, testimony-building experiences within that environment.

So, whether their children are born with genetic disorders or minds filled with anger, most parents have to deal with difficult, inborn attributes brought about by genetic selection. We need to understand that we were not blessed or cursed by God as we became parents. The difficulties that come with children are a part of our mortal probation on this earth. As it turns out, parenting is a risky as well as difficult business.

EPIGENETICS

As just mentioned, we are more than our genetic makeup. There is a regulating process built into your DNA to help it adapt to the choices that you make. In a developing field called "epigenetics," scientists are discovering how our genes can be activated or deactivated by outside influences, especially choices in lifestyle. For example, if both of your parents are obese, you may think it inevitable that you will be obese as well. It is true that those genes will influence your body shape, but if you live a healthy lifestyle, maintain a reduced caloric intake, and exercise, some of the genes that build fat cells will actually be "turned off" by your body. Thus, by self-control, you can suppress the genes that lead to increased obesity. The *lifestyle decisions you make in your life* (diet, physical activity, stress levels, sleep, social activity, etc.) have a significant effect on which genes are expressed. You are not just a product of your chromosomes. Your body allows you to tweak your genetic programming to be closer to the person you want to be.

In his book *The Developing Genome*, David S. Moore concludes,

> Our characteristics develop because of the mutual activities of a variety of genetic, epigenetic, and environmental factors *that operate as an integrated system.* Our traits are not predetermined by any single factor; we are more than our biological endowments . . . That is an important message, because

it can help us resist the illusion that we have no control over who and how we are. What we do matters.[8]

THE ADVANTAGES OF RANDOMNESS

From our earthly understanding of them, life and genetics do not seem at all "fair" in their assignment of bodies to the children who are born onto earth. One child will be born into a wealthy family in a prosperous country. Another child will join a family that lives in the poorest region of a third-world country. The next child will be born with genetic issues that will severely limit her physical and mental development. Many people don't cope well with the randomness of this selection process and look for meaning behind each birth, but genetics teaches us that randomness is one of the facts of earth life. As discussed, when the DNA of your parents come together to make your body, each of the twenty thousand selections of genes appears to be completely random. Many important events of your life, such as tragic accidents, meeting someone who will become a lifelong friend or spouse, and job opportunities, appear to be random chance as well.

Though Christians will often look for God's hand behind these random events, most of them probably do happen by chance. The problem with thinking that God manipulates and directs each moment of our lives is that soon we become like puppets in a play. By that theory, we never really had agency. In the Final Judgment, I can claim that I cannot be judged for my poor decisions because God put especially hard challenges on my path that led me to a poor ending. I can point out that God put a wonderful spouse, obedient children, and amazing job opportunities in the path of my wealthy friend Tim. Tim then cruised through life and church activity. How is that fair? You may argue that Tim was more righteous than I and received more blessings because of it. But that response gets us right back into the Book of Job argument of whether God's blessings come in proportion to our righteousness. Like Job, there are far too many examples of righteous people who have been afflicted with severe difficulties to ever win that debate. With my comparison to Tim, I could legitimately question the fairness of a telestial judgment. To summarize, there are many difficulties in believing the Final Judgment can be fair if God chooses and provides my spouse, my children, my job opportunities, and my health.

However, these difficulties disappear if life is random. Randomness may be unpredictable and cruel at times, but it is fair. If you have an extra ticket to the baseball game and five friends want to go with you, the fairest thing for you to do is draw straws or pick numbers from a hat. Both are random selections, so your friends cannot claim you were unfair or favored one of them over another. God cannot play favorites, since, once again, it does not allow for fair and righteous judgments. However, we are told that, in the end, we will all recognize that the Final Judgment was just (Mosiah 16:1). Though you may agonize at the thought that it has a great effect on your life, randomness may actually play a major role in assuring that fairness.

As well it should, our society recognizes the determination of those people who started life in poverty and were able to achieve financial success. We also admire those who have been born or thrust into disability but then go on to rise above their handicaps to live exemplary and successful lives. The accomplishments of Helen Keller, Franklin Delano Roosevelt, Stevie Wonder, and Stephen Hawking will be remembered for many years to come. In conclusion, we may have no control over the cards we are dealt in life, but each of us gets to decide how to play those cards to live good lives, attain wisdom, and choose righteousness, thus winning the game.

Chapter 9

Rule 5: Temporal Life Must Be Temporary

WE LIVE IN A TEMPORAL WORLD, meaning this world is secular as opposed to spiritual. It is also a *temporary* world as opposed to a permanent one. Nothing that physically exists in this world is meant to last forever. Paint peels, metals rust, mountains erode away, and all living things die. Decay and death are a part of life, yet many people are angry with God because of that inevitability. But there are good reasons for aging, breakdown, and death—reasons that justify our heartache as our keepsakes decay and our loved ones die. As we will see, older generations must pass away to make room for the new.

Wood Rots

Wood is by far the most versatile building material. It allowed explorers to build the ships that took them to foreign, unexplored lands. For thousands of years wood has made up the supporting structures of our homes. Without trees and the lumber they provide, our homes would have to be made of dirt, bricks, and stones. However, wood comes with disadvantages. It rots. Wood is broken down and eaten by fungi, termites, and carpenter ants.[1, 2] Homeowners spend billions of dollars each year to protect their homes from water and pests. Wood also burns. Fighting wildfires in the U.S. cost over two billion dollars in 2017.[3] Fighting structural fires cost American home and business owners eighty-nine billion in 2014.[4] Couldn't wood be more impervious to such problems? Fortunately, it is not.

About 250 million years ago, certain small plants evolved the ability to internally produce a sturdy, long-chain polymer called cellulose.[5] By stacking and bonding cellulose fibers together to form wood, these plants were able to form the internal scaffolding needed to grow taller than competing plants and access more sunlight. The early trees were coniferous, the ancestors of our pine, spruce, and fir trees today. This height advantage allowed trees to survive ice ages and other environmental changes. Trees continued to evolve and grew even taller to better ensure their access to sunlight.

If there are no forest fires or other natural disasters, trees can live for many years. Some trees, such as palm varieties, live only forty to fifty years, but the California redwood can live up to two thousand years, and the bristlecone pine can live up to five thousand years. Eventually, however, the cambium, or living tissue of the tree, clogs up and wears out. Water and minerals cannot ascend from the roots, and sugars made in the leaves cannot descend. Simple weathering causes bark to fall off. At some point, the tree dies and stops combatting the forces that are working to destroy it. The wood dries out, and stress cracks begin to appear. Finally, the tree weakens so much that it is toppled by the next stiff wind.

If there were no decay, that first tree that ever died would still be lying on the ground today. A second generation of trees would have sprung up around the log, lived their life spans, and fallen to earth as well. Third, fourth, and fifth generations would have done the same. So if trees evolved 250 million years ago and a generation of trees lives an average of a thousand years, about 250,000 generations of trees could be lying on the ground today. Our forests would be very large piles of dead wood, blocking all sunlight from reaching the ground. Woodlands would have no new growth, leaves, berries, nuts, or fruit. No animal life could be sustained. Vast tracts of the earth would be dead and unusable.

So thank goodness for decay. When a tree falls, small cellulose demolition crews soon arrive. In a wet, humid environment, bacteria thrive, breaking down cellulose on a microscopic level. Fungal spores, including brown rot, white rot, bird nest, and other mushrooms arrive on the wind and sprout on the decaying wood. Termites, carpenter ants, and other wood-boring insects infest the log. Decay is slow, and sometimes nature will resort to faster methods. If there is a lot of dead wood lying on the ground, forest fires (started by lightening or careless hikers) will rage through those woodlands, clearing the ground for new growth. Whether by decay or fire, bits and pieces of the old wood fall onto the ground and become the mulch that gives volume and richness to the soil. Seeds find both space and fertile ground from which to sprout.

When life was first created, God commanded that every species be fruitful and multiply. The earth was commanded to bring forth grass, herbs, and fruits (Genesis 1:11), and later cattle, creeping things, and beasts of the earth (Genesis 1:24). The waters were commanded to bring forth sea creatures, fish, and birds (Genesis 1:20). Genesis reports the creation of man in Genesis 1:27 and man was commanded to be fruitful and multiply in the *following verse*. Thus, from the beginning, life has been linked with reproduction, but reproduction requires that older generations pass away to make space for the new arrivals. In the case of trees (and all other plants as well), destruction by bacteria, fungi, insects, and fire are in place to remove past generations to make room for new generations. Wherever there is corporeal life and reproduction, death and decay must exist as well.

Sadie the Perfect Dog

When my children were still children, we adopted a female golden retriever puppy and named her Sadie. Sadie lived her whole life with our family. Most Sundays, we would go on family walks, and Sadie would always accompany us, getting visibly upset when our children ran, rollerbladed, or biked ahead. She wrestled, retrieved, and ran with our children. Sadie had a (planned) litter of puppies, and she was a great mom. When Sadie turned twelve years old, she started to gray and slow down. She gradually became arthritic and had a hard time rising from her favorite spot in the family room. A couple of years later, to her horror and embarrassment, Sadie lost control of her bladder. She was in a lot of pain, and I finally took her to her veterinarian to be euthanized. It was the hardest thing I have ever done in my life.

Our grown children still quite seriously refer to Sadie as the perfect dog. It is a fair assessment. Sadie lived the perfect dog life. She taught us to love animals, grieve without judgment, be gentle with others, and enjoy a simple run through the yard. It is a sad fact that pets do not have the same life span as humans. They come into our lives, make their impact on us, and then pass away. There is wisdom in this process. We know that animals fear death. They too have a desire for self-preservation. They too have a fight or flight response to danger. But most animals are willing to give their lives in defense of their young. I think if we could ask our pets if they are willing to die of old age to make room for their next generations, they would agree to the need. I know Sadie would have.

OUR BODIES ARE TEMPORARY VEHICLES

The most distressing aspect of the fact that we live in a temporal world is realizing that we are temporary too. Actually, humans are one of the most long-lived species on earth. Only a few animals, such as tortoises, sea urchins, and bowhead whales, live longer. This is small comfort. Though inevitable, aging and death are considered two of the great tragedies of life. The fact of the matter is—we hate aging. There are many sayings that indicate our disdain for old age. You should be "young at heart," "forty is the new thirty," and then "fifty is the new thirty." My personal favorite is, "I'm not going to age gracefully. I'm going to fight it every step of the way."

But the declaration "Turning fifty, looking thirty, feeling twenty" probably best summarizes our feelings about aging. We don't *feel* old, and we try our best *not to look* old. Since we don't feel or look old, we are often shocked when our bodies start breaking down. We may ask the Lord, "Why me?" when the answer is obvious. We hate the answer—you are getting old and your turn on earth is almost over. If you are in denial of anything in this world, it is probably the approach of death. In discussing the rules of earth, it seems appropriate to recognize that the infirmities of old age and death are included in those rules.

SCRIPTURAL EVIDENCE THAT LIFE IS MEANT TO BE TEMPORARY

In the Garden of Eden, Adam and Eve partook of the fruit of the tree of knowledge of good and evil but were not permitted to partake of the fruit of the tree of life. In fact, it was so important to the Lord to keep Adam and Eve away from the tree of life that He drove them out of the Garden of Eden *and* placed "Cherubims, and a flaming sword which turned every way" to guard the tree (Genesis 3:24). A lot of symbolism should probably be attached to this verse, but it appears that the Lord was serious about keeping men's sojourn on earth a temporary event. Alma supports this conclusion in his long discussion with his son Corianton:

> For behold, if Adam had put forth his hand immediately, and partaken of the tree of life, he would have lived forever, according to the word of God, having no space for repentance; yea, and also the word of God would have been void, and the great plan of salvation would have been frustrated . . . Now behold, it was not expedient that man should be reclaimed from this temporal death, for that would destroy the great plan of happiness. (Alma 42:5, 8)

So, given that life is temporary, can we hope to live as long as Adam? In this book, we will not try to guess why the Old Testament reports such high ages for the early patriarchs. Adam reportedly lived to be 930 (Genesis 5:5) and Methuselah to 969 (Genesis 5:27). According to Genesis 9:29, Noah lived to be 950 years old. All begat children well after the age of 100. But after Noah, the reported ages of succeeding generations began to decrease. Abraham lived 175 years (Genesis 25:7), while his great-grandson Joseph only lived to 110 (Genesis 50:22). But this is a discussion that is better left for another day. In summary, no one in this life gets to be another Methuselah. If they ever existed, the days of living for almost a millennium are past.

A Psalm attributed to Moses states,

> The days of our years are three-score and ten; and if by reason of strength they be fourscore years, yet is their strength labor and sorrow; for it is soon cut off, and we fly away. (Psalms 90:10)

Moses states that a normal life span is seventy years, and, if we make it to eighty years, we can expect death to take us soon. This is the same longevity that we have today. It is believed that Moses was born about 1400 BC, so apparently mankind has had about the same expected life span for 3400 years.

Medical Evidence That Our Bodies Are Meant to Be Temporary

A graph of increasing life expectancy over the past decades could lead to the expectation that there is no limit to how long we might eventually live. In fact, some people think that medicine will eventually conquer death so that mankind can enjoy endless years of life. For a large fee you can have your entire body or just your brain frozen until the time medical science has discovered the way to thaw you out and keep you alive. However compelling the idea of living for hundreds of years may be, there is little evidence that it is possible.

In truth, average life expectancy has been on the rise for over a hundred years now. In 1900, the average life span was forty-eight years. By 1950, life expectancy had increased to sixty-four years. In 2012, the Center for Disease Control announced that life expectancy in the USA had hit 78.8 years—a record high.[6] However, most all of this increase can be attributed to much-improved neonatal survival and disease prevention. Our *longevity*, or how long you can live barring plague, accidental death, wars, or lightning strikes has not increased that significantly. The first English child born in Massachusetts in 1621 lived until she was ninety-six. The longest-lived documented human being in history was a French woman named Madame Jeanne Calment who was born in 1875 and lived until she was 122.[7] Despite the continued improvements in health care and disease prevention, adult life spans have not increased significantly for hundreds of years. Despite the speculations of science fiction writers, it appears that the human life span has a natural limit. A book written about the subject states,

> Whether the result of wear, tear, and exhaustion of resources or whether genetically programmed, all life has a finite span and each species has its own particular longevity. . . . Though biomedical science has vastly increased mankind's *average* life expectancy, the *maximum* has not changed in verifiable recorded history. In developed countries, only one in ten thousand people lives beyond the age of one hundred.[8]

A recent study on the matter concluded, "Hence, in contrast to previous suggestions that human longevity can be extended even further, our data strongly suggests that the duration of life is limited."[9]

YOUR DNA, LIFESTYLE, AND LONGEVITY

Your personal life span is mostly set by two variables. The first, which you can't control, is your genetics. Fortunately, our DNA (or Deoxyribonucleic acid) gives us many years of life in comparison to other species. Fruit flies only live twenty-one days. Mice only live for three years. The largest dog breeds normally live to about twelve years old, while smaller dogs can live twice that long. So it seems obvious that aging is determined to a large extent by your DNA. There are several theories as to how cells age, most of which have to do with the cell reproduction process. Cells in your body have to divide and multiply regularly. For example, the lining of your stomach replaces itself every five days.[10] Your skin regenerates itself about every twenty-seven days.[11] With each division, your DNA strands have to unravel, reproduce themselves to provide a copy for the new cell, and then reestablish the double helix. One of the most recent and persuasive models that connects DNA with aging is based on "telomeres," or the DNA segments on the very end of each helical strand. These end-caps are specially structured to be the starting point for the DNA copying process. Sometimes the copying process does not start at the very end of the original DNA, so the telomeres of the copy are not as long as those of the original. This shortening process continues in succeeding generations of cells. When the telomeres of a helix get too short, the DNA strand cannot copy itself and the cell dies. Apparently, our cells have the ability to add to the telomere sequences, but this rebuilding process cannot keep up with the deterioration. As we get older, the telomeres in your cells' DNA get shorter. More cell death occurs, which strains the body as it works to clear the dead cells and replace them. On a cellular level, all functions of your body start to show signs of aging.[12]

The second variable that affects your longevity is your lifestyle. Do you remember your doctor's advice at each annual checkup? He probably recommends that you eat smaller portions of healthy foods, reduce stress, get a good night's sleep, and exercise more. You should pay attention to this wise man's advice, because not taking your doctor's advice will usually lead to a shorter life. Granted, there are times when genetics can trump lifestyle. For example, Madame Jeanne, the longest-lived person in modern history, smoked until she was 117.[13] Obviously, Madame's DNA was very resistant to cancer, but betting that your genetics will effectively triumph over poor lifestyle decisions has its risks. Like your DNA, your lifestyle choices also affect you all the way down to your cells. As the actress Cameron Diaz explains in her book on the subject:

> Along the course of a healthy lifetime, your body is in a constant state of transformation, renewal, and rebirth at the most microscopic level. Your health begins with your cells. Every sign of aging you see and feel on the surface, every sag and wrinkle and pain, begins in your cells. They are

> dynamic and responsive to your environment, to your stress levels, to your nutrition, and to the prompts of your hormones and the expression of your genes.[14]

Stress is a good example of how the outside world affects you on the cellular level. Adrenaline and norepinephrine are largely responsible for the immediate reactions we feel when stressed. Both surge quickly when we are anxious, afraid, or angered. Cortisol is a slower stress hormone that illustrates the complexity of our body's reactions to external threat. In order of sequence, the part of the brain called the amygdala recognizes a threat and sends a message to another part of the brain called the hypothalamus. The hypothalamus releases "corticotropin-releasing hormone," which tells the pituitary gland to release "adrenocorticotropic hormone," which tells the adrenal glands to produce cortisol. All three of these hormones put your body on high alert. You feel a surge of energy, increased mental focus, and an accelerated heart rate to provide more oxygen to your muscles. You become primed to fight, flee, argue, or deal with a difficult work assignment, calm an angry neighbor, or defuse any other threat. But there is a cost to your body for this hormone rush. Your body must eventually work its way down from its high-alert/high-stress status. This whole process takes its toll on the cells in your brain, heart, and other organs, which partially explains why you are tired after a stressful day.

If aging really occurs as the DNA programming in our cells starts to unravel, then one might expect our body systems to all start shutting down at the same time. This is exactly what happens. In his book, *Being Mortal*, Dr. Atul Gawande explains,

> Old age is not a diagnosis. There is always some final proximate cause that gets written down on the death certificate—respiratory failure, cardiac arrest. But in truth no single disease leads to the end; the culprit is just the accumulated crumbling of one's body systems while medicine carries out its maintenance measures and patch jobs.[15]

No one dies of old age—you die from the *complications* of old age. Each individual system of your body gradually shuts down, gradually weakening the whole. For example, though eating and digestion seem simple enough, it is a complex process with many steps—all of which can break down. Your teeth gradually lose their enamel and their blood supply atrophies, causing you to lose your teeth. At the same time, the muscles in your jaws weaken and loose mass, further reducing your ability to chew.

The muscles of our digestive system weaken, so food moves more slowly though the colon, often causing constipation.

Hormone production in elderly bodies is reduced, which leads to numerous problems, not the least of which is osteoporosis and the weakening of bones. Cholesterol and triglycerides in your blood form plaque deposits on the walls of your arteries, restricting blood flow. Calcium deposits also accumulate on artery walls and heart muscle and valves, causing them to stiffen and lose elasticity. Between the plaque and calcium, the heart has to generate more pressure to get the blood to flow through these narrower veins, leading to hypertension. Calcium also accumulates in the lungs, reducing their capacity. Thus, climbing a flight of stairs leaves us both flushed and breathless. We lose cartilage from all our joints, causing bone-on-bone contact and constant pain. Finally, our brains actually shrink, and our mental capacity shrinks with it. At thirty, the brain fills up the cranium. By seventy, there is an extra inch of spare room.[16]

It's Time to Move On

Life seems to help us prepare for each new step in our life's plan. A good example is found in our roles of being a parent. When our children are preteen, they are so cute, pleasant, loving, and fun that we could not imagine life without them. The thought of them going off to college and to lives of their own is heartbreaking. But as our children grow older and become teenagers, they need more independence. Hormones to prepare them for their lives as adults start to kick in. The developing young adult becomes more difficult, impatient, disobedient, and even angry. Arguments with siblings become more frequent. The transformation is heartbreaking—but it also helps to prepare parents for the eventual separation. By the time their daughter is fifteen or so, her parents may begin to think that maybe it won't be so bad for her to be off on her own. By the time the daughter is, say, seventeen, her parents may start actually looking forward to the peace and harmony that will come from having their daughter away at college. Having a child graduate from high school and leave home is still difficult, but life has a way of preparing us for this next stage of our lives—we just have to be aware that it is going on.

As you get older, your body is desperately trying to tell you something. As explained by author Sherwin Nuland,

> Old age is the preparation for departure, the gradual easing out of life that makes its ending more palatable not only for those who are elderly but for those to whom they leave the world in trust.[17]

Life on earth should be wonderful. We love our earthly lives and our families, and we never want to leave. But the pains of old age, the frustration of losing our mental acuteness, and perpetual exhaustion all have their effect. Perhaps these difficulties should not be seen as a curse but more as a kindly reminder. We are being given fair warning that our time is about up. It is a transition that we may fear, but the pain of those last years can help us understand that maybe it won't be so bad to move on to the next plane of existence. We can slowly release our desperate grip on our life. Children and grandchildren can also witness the deterioration of their loved ones and understand that death may be a release rather than a tragedy.

One of the greatest expressions of a strong testimony of the gospel of Jesus Christ is being able to look into the face of death with no fear. If you truly believe in eternal life, death is just a portal. Yes, the portal is one-way and you will miss the people you must leave behind. You have been separated from loved ones before. Fear of death is mostly just a fear of the unknown. If you have a strong testimony of the Savior, then you must also believe in the resurrection. Otherwise, what is the point of the gospel? In the end, the largest "leap of faith" we will ever take in life is accepting death.

Chapter 10

Rule 6: We Must Suffer the Consequences of Others' Bad Decisions

In this world, there are two types of bad decisions for which you must suffer. In chapter 2, we learned that you must suffer for your own bad decisions. For example, you can decide to ignore a stop sign and get into an auto accident. The collision was your fault, and you will suffer—possibly in bodily injury and certainly financially. But on earth you must also suffer for the decisions of *other people*. Someone else may decide to ignore a stop sign and get into an accident with you. The collision was *not* your fault, but you will still suffer—possibly in bodily injury or even death.

We know very little about the premortal existence, but we do have evidence that we suffered for our own bad decisions while there. In the premortal existence, a number of our spiritual brethren decided to rebel against Heavenly Father's plan for earth life and eternal progression. It was a poor decision on their part—and they are suffering the consequences.

> And it came to pass that Adam, being tempted of the devil—for, behold, the devil was before Adam, for he rebelled against me, saying, Give me thine honor, which is my power; and also a third part of the hosts of heaven turned he away from me because of their agency; And they were thrust down, and thus came the devil and his angels. (D&C 29:36–37)

It seems logical and fair that if we use our agency to make decisions, we are responsible for those decisions in any realm. It is part of the learning process. Though we don't know our options there, we had agency in the premortal existence. We were apparently allowed to make certain decisions and suffer the consequences of the bad ones.

But even with a limited vision of the premortal existence, there is no evidence that we had to suffer the consequences of *other* people's decisions while there. For example, on earth we could be injured in a car accident with a drunk driver. In the premortal existence, such a life-rattling event doesn't seem possible because

1. I don't think there is alcohol in the premortal existence.
2. Without a body, it seems unlikely anyone could get drunk in the premortal existence anyway.
3. There is no scriptural evidence that we drove cars in the premortal existence.
4. Most important, could spiritual bodies even be injured in a car accident?

In a spiritual existence, it seems unlikely we had to suffer severe consequences for the poor decisions of other people. There is no evidence that a spiritual body can be harmed, but when we came to Earth, we were given breakable mortal bodies. We now live in a place where other people can damage us physically, mentally, and emotionally. The rules changed. Our spiritual brothers and sisters could now hurt us, either accidently or with intent, or even end our mortal lives.

THE BAD DECISIONS OF FAMILY

At the beginning of life, we necessarily surround ourselves with people called "family." These people have the power to affect our lives. We love our family and we feel a responsibility for them. Almost always, they are a vital support to our early years and well into adulthood. Sometimes they are not. Childhood is a difficult time. We are trying to establish our own identities and learn to socialize with those around us. We learn to rely on our family members to help us deal with life. When we marry, we adopt a whole other family of in-laws that we look to for help.

Family members who died long ago have even affected our lives. The country in which you were born was determined by the ancestors who chose to immigrate to your country of birth. Who your great-grandfather chose to marry determined about 12.5 percent of your DNA. Your parents decided where you would spend the first couple of decades of your life. Childhood is the time of life when you have the least amount of agency. Your parents have the responsibility to make major decisions for you until you are legally an adult, usually at age eighteen. We all have childhood experiences that affect us into adulthood. I have a scar on my head that I can blame on my mother (auto accident) and my brother has one he can blame on me (frozen snowball). Other people suffer from more serious scars that are emotional in nature.

Afflictions caused by those we love are especially painful. If your parents decide to separate, or your spouse decides to dissolve your marriage, or a child moves out unexpectedly, you are left with the pain of separation without having a voice in the decision. Not surprisingly, your hopes and plans do not always align with those you love. A marriage can only stay in place if both spouses agree to the arrangement. A family of five can remain close only if all five members choose to do so. As one's family gets larger, the probability of losing someone grows proportionally. There are many sad stories about close families that became dysfunctional because of the choices of one member.

Having the agency to make decisions is *great* when it applies to me, but must I extend the same right to my children and grandchildren? I am told I must, but it is certainly not my first choice. When others, especially my loved ones, make decisions that make my life sadder or more difficult, I am no longer a big fan of the whole agency concept. If I have an errant son, I pray to God to "soften his heart," but I'm hoping for an intervention similar to that provided to Alma the Younger in the Book of Mormon.

To set the stage for this account, Alma the Elder was the chief judge and high priest of the Nephite people. His son and namesake, Alma the Younger, had become "a very wicked and an adulterous man." He had led many of his people away from the Church and went about "causing much dissension about the people."

> And as I said unto you, as they were going about rebelling against God, behold, the angel of the Lord appeared unto them; and he descended as it were in a cloud; and he spake as it were with a voice of thunder, which caused the earth to shake upon which they stood;
>
> And again, the angel said: Behold, the Lord hath heard the prayers of his people, and also the prayers of his servant, Alma, who is thy father; for he has prayed with much faith concerning thee that thou mightest be brought

> to the knowledge of the truth; therefore, for this purpose have I come to convince thee of the power and authority of God, that the prayers of his servants might be answered according to their faith.
>
> And now behold, can ye dispute the power of God? For behold, doth not my voice shake the earth? And can ye not also behold me before you? And I am sent from God. (Mosiah 27:11, 14, 15)

After reading these verses, I think all parents of wayward children may pray, *"Dear Heavenly Father, in regard to my troubled son, I would like to refer you to Mosiah 27. You probably know the angel that appeared to Alma the Younger, whose voice shook the ground. Could you please send that same angel to appear to my son and have him deliver the same message? I think that is what it will take to get him to listen . . ."*

Wouldn't such an intervention be wonderful? Unfortunately, this is the only example in the scriptures of an angel appearing to an errant son at the request of a parent. Maybe it was because Alma the Younger was using his relationship to the prophet to do real damage to the Church. Angelic visitations are rare. This rule of earth demands that each person's agency be respected. It is the only way we learn.

THE BAD DECISIONS OF FRIENDS AND STRANGERS

If you chose to live by yourself on a small deserted island in the South Pacific, you would probably not have to suffer from other people's decisions. As distressing as it is to think about, the decisions of total strangers can affect our lives. We suffer when someone around us chooses not to be careful, be that another driver, another player in your pickup basketball game, or another shopper breezing through a door at the mall. We call these injuries "accidents," since the responsible person did not intentionally mean to hurt you. But, let's face it, most accidents result from bad decisions. Some drivers think that they can eat a sandwich, text on their phone, and drive on a highway all at the same time. When they crash into someone, it is still called an accident. Often the guilty party walks away unscathed, leaving the injured party to deal with pain, suffering, and surgery for years to come. Such victims need to understand that their first reaction to this reality—"THIS IS NOT FAIR!"—is inarguably correct. Many people spend their lives angry at the injustice of losing loved ones, possessions, or investments due to the decisions of others. Though we have been promised that everyone will eventually be judged and that justice will be restored, those corrections will probably not happen until the next life (Alma 41:4). We have no promise that justice in this earthly existence will be swift.

I have read numerous articles that declare that you should enjoy, even cherish, your trials and challenges. This is an overstatement. Such a belief rather supports masochism for yourself and sadism to "help" other people have more trials to enjoy. Trials at work, personal injury, loved ones making bad decisions, and other challenges are not meant to be enjoyed. The goal is to patiently suffer through them and, it is hoped, emerge from the experience a stronger *and wiser* person.

But the intent of this book is not simply to console and encourage those people who have passed through a trial. The goal of this book is to help the reader understand the rules of this earth life. We are in this life as groups—families, neighborhoods, ward congregations, cities, states, countries, church, and earthlings. The scriptures teach us time and again that we are here to learn to support one another. In all that human interaction, one person can make a bad decision whose consequences are shared by family and friends. That fact does not make life fairer, but it is a reason why we are here. We are, literally, all in this together.

THE BAD DECISIONS OF LEADERS

To better illustrate the rules of earth, we have been reviewing the most extreme examples of how each rule has been applied in Earth's history. The best examples of suffering the consequences of others' decisions are found in the decisions of our world leaders. Bad decisions by the leader of a group will almost always negatively affect *every* member of the group. We hope that our leaders, be they in our workplace, government, or religion, make decisions that are best for the majority of their followers. But that does not always happen.

In the premortal existence, our family head and government leader was Heavenly Father, who didn't make any bad decisions as far as I know. We do know that there were noble and great spirits who were recognized and selected to be leaders on this earth (D&C 138: 55–56). However, I don't know of any scriptures that indicate the noble and great ones had authority over us in the premortal existence. Though the scriptures do indicate that the Savior and Satan were highly favored, it does not appear that they had leadership titles. If there had been an established hierarchy, Heavenly Father would probably have not had to ask, "Whom shall I send?" In the same scripture, it does not appear that Satan had any followers either until he decided to rebel.

> And the Lord said: *Whom shall I send?* And one answered like unto the Son of Man: Here am I, send me. And another answered and said: Here am I, send me. And the Lord said: I will send the first. And the second was angry, and kept not his first estate; and, *at that day*, many followed after him. (Abraham 3:27; italics added)

So it appears that suffering the consequences of bad decisions by leaders is probably another part of earth life that we did not have to experience in the premortal existence.

The Book of Mormon, especially King Mosiah, has a lot to say about forms of government. As Mosiah's reign was ending, the Nephite people wanted Mosiah's son Aaron to become their new king (Mosiah 29). But neither Aaron nor any of his brothers wanted to be king, preferring to do missionary work among the Lamanites. So, Mosiah sent out an epistle to his people to suggest that they adopt a new form of government. In Mosiah 29:13, the retiring King Mosiah admits that "if it were possible that you could have just men to be your kings . . . then it would be expedient that ye should always have kings to rule over you." In truth, a just king really is the safest and most efficient form of government. It means you will have a good and just man leading his people along the paths of righteousness. There is no need for the bother and delays of counting votes to make every decision. One righteous man makes all decisions immediately, and he always makes them for the benefit of his subjects.

However, Mosiah petitioned his people to reject the idea of having a king. His argument was that having a king is just too dangerous.

> Now I say unto you, that because all men are not just it is not expedient that ye should have a king or kings to rule over you. For behold, how much iniquity doth one wicked king cause to be committed, yea, and what great destruction! Yea, remember king Noah, his wickedness and his abominations, and also the wickedness and abominations of his people. Behold what great destruction did come upon them; and also because of their iniquities they were brought into bondage. (Mosiah 29:16–18)

Even if you have a righteous king, he will eventually have to pass the kingdom on to the next generation, usually one of his sons. Until democracy, the populace never had a say in the choice of their new rulers. Mosiah's example of King Noah illustrates this problem quite well. King Zeniff, though admittedly over-zealous to inherit the land of his fathers (Mosiah 9:3), seemed to be a caring king. The same could not be said of his son, Noah, who was a wicked man who caused much grief among his people. Mosiah warned his people of a truth that would be restated almost two thousand years later to Joseph Smith while he was imprisoned in Liberty Jail. While it is a beautifully written verse, I have always found this scripture to be more than a little depressing.

> We have learned by sad experience that it is the nature and disposition of almost all men, as soon as they get a little authority, as they suppose, they will immediately begin to exercise unrighteous dominion. (D&C 121:39)

To continue the narrative, Mosiah did not want the Nephites to have to suffer for the selfish, unrighteous decisions of a king. He asked them to adopt a form of democracy and spread the power to rule over a group of judges, who would be voted into office by the voice of the people.

> Therefore, choose you by the voice of the people, judges, that ye may be judged according to the laws which have been given you by your fathers, which are correct, and which were given them by the hand of the Lord. (Mosiah 29:25)

In Mosiah 28:28–29, it is explained that the higher judges could overturn the rulings of these elected judges if necessary. Conversely, the rulings of a higher judge could be overturned by a group of lower judges. Thus, if one evil man managed to become a judge, other judges could control his self-serving rulings and ambition. Mosiah knew bloody revolutions were required for a people to replace a poor king, but if judges could be elected by the voice of the people, then bad judges could be changed out by simple election. Since judges could overrule each other, they were set to watch over each other to prevent abuses. The democratic republic of the United States of America is built upon this foundation and principle. Democratic elections were designed to allow the removal of poor leaders.

Unfortunately, democracy is not a foolproof system. While no one thinks they are electing wicked men into office, such elections happen. In the history of the world, some truly awful kings, emperors, czars, and presidents have exercised unrighteous dominion. These men have brought much suffering into the world. To best illustrate the suffering that has come from allowing evil men to take power over governments, we will discuss two of the very worst—Adolf Hitler and Joseph Stalin. If God was ever going to step in and remove two world leaders from office and mortality, it would have been these two men. But mankind had to be allowed to make horrendously bad decisions to learn some very important principles. The consequences of allowing evil men to lead your government are severe. Adolf Hitler and Joseph Stalin came to power because the people of Germany and Russia, respectively, allowed them to do so. As we will see, voters who are angry and frustrated can elect malicious leaders into office. Such citizens are desperate for change, whether it hurts other people or not. But in the end, this attitude is destructive. Germany and Russia paid a high price for decisions made almost a century ago.

As the saying goes, "Those who do not learn from their past are doomed to repeat it." We need to realize that God will let such devastations happen again if the people of a country decide to allow it. Thus, in this discussion, we will review not only the actions of dishonorable leaders themselves, but also the citizens of the countries that allowed them into power in the first place.

GERMANY AND NAZISM

Germany is a beautiful country and the Germans are a very industrious, hardworking people. It was the homeland of many prominent scientists throughout history, including Albert Einstein, Max Planck, Johannes Kepler, and Carl Friedrich Gauss. Germany was the birthplace of some of the major pharmaceutical and chemical manufacturers in the world. It is perplexing that such an advanced country could have made such poor decisions in the first half of the 1900s.

On August 1, 1914, Germany entered World War I by declaring war on Russia and then France. By the time World War I ended in November 1918, Germany had lost the war, over 2,000,000 fighting men, and 913,000 civilians.[1] The German people were both astonished and humiliated that their beloved country had lost the Great War. Many blamed the German chancellor for poor leadership and a premature surrender. In January 1919, leaders of Great Britain, France, and the United States met to determine the fate of the defeated powers. The resulting Treaty of Versailles established sanctions against Germany to prevent it from gathering the resources to ever launch war again. Germany was directed to give up lands, agree to military occupation, restrict its own armed forces, and to pay huge economic reparations to the victorious countries. Historians now recognize that the conditions of the Treaty of Versailles were overly demanding. Germany did not have the resources to pay the billions of German marks required by the victors for reparations. Germany's citizens chafed against the harsh restrictions that would demand years of sacrifice from them.

In 1924, the German economy collapsed.[2] Inflation had made the German mark worthless. In the course of a few months, elderly citizens saw their entire retirement savings disappear. In 1929, the onset of the Great Depression in the United States crippled the struggling economy in Germany even further. American banks had provided loans to a number of German companies to help them recover. To deal with their own financial meltdown in America, those loans were recalled. German businesses closed and unemployment soared. In the course of only fifteen years, Germany went from a prosperous nation to mass unemployment, hunger, and chaos. The German people were humiliated, angry, frustrated, and saw no hope of recovery. Such emotions do not often lend themselves to making good decisions. The German people wanted drastic change all too desperately.

In 1919, Adolf Hitler had joined what became the German Worker's Party, a radically socialist party built on the premise that Germans were a superior race and that Jews, Communists, and other non-Germans had caused the mistakes and horrors of the last two decades. This message appealed to the populace. By this logic, Germany was not at fault for its massively bad decisions. German woes could be blamed on minorities and immigrants that they distrusted anyway. They had a scapegoat. By 1921, Hitler became the acknowledged leader of the Worker's Party, which later became the Nazi party. By 1928, membership in the party stood at one hundred thousand members. In the elections of 1932, the Nazi party took control of the Reichstag Parliament. As the leader of that party (and in an effort by moderates to keep him under control), Hitler was appointed as chancellor of all Germany. It was at this point that the German people lost control of their future. With the death of German president Paul von Hindenburg in 1934, Adolf Hitler made himself both chancellor and president, giving himself the new title of Fuhrer. By August of 1939, Hitler invaded Poland, which started World War II. It should be noted that the Germans were not alone in this war of aggression. Italy had allowed Benito Mussolini to become dictator and join Hitler in his efforts. Tojo Hideki became the prime minister of Japan in October 1941. Two months later, the attack on Pearl Harbor was launched with the end goal of establishing a new Japanese empire in China, Australia, and Southeast Asia.[3] Hitler was not alone in his grab for power over the lives of millions.

There is no need to list the atrocities of World War II. Suffice it to say that sixty to seventy million people died in the war, including soldiers and civilians of nearly every corner of the world.[4] The German people, by supporting the rise of the Nazi party into power, had unwittingly put themselves on a path that would lead to the near destruction of their county and the deaths of millions of their countrymen. With the authority given him, Hitler made decisions that affected every corner of the world. My father-in-law, Jack Sakdol, living peacefully in Kansas, joined the U.S. Navy when he was seventeen years old to fight the Japanese in the Pacific Theatre. The decisions of Adolf Hitler and Tojo Hideki reached around the globe and changed my father-in-law's life forever. So we learn that the poor decisions of just a few world leaders can plunge the entire world into a brutal war.

Interestingly, we also learn that the poor decisions of just a few world leaders can also reach across time itself to affect millions.

Russia and Communism

Like Germany, by early 1917, Russia had endured over two years of World War I. Troop loss was high and food supplies had dwindled in the major cities. For three hundred years, Russia had been governed by the Czar dynasty of the house of Romanov, but citizens considered the Czar to be both outdated and autocratic. Like Germany, the Russian people were losing a war, going hungry at home, and desperately trying to get an unresponsive government to help. Finally, the citizenry rebelled. The Russian revolution started with waves of strikes and demonstrations in the capital Petrograd (now St. Petersburg). When it appeared that the military would soon join the rebellion, Czar Nicholas II abdicated the throne and a provisional government was put into place.[5]

But the Russian people were no longer willing to be governed by a central government. Local "soviets" or councils of workers and soldiers sprang up across the country to make their own laws. As the provisional government tried to establish order, conditions deteriorated further. In July 1917, the new government, hoping to demonstrate strength and re-establish the war effort, ordered a military offensive against enemy forces in Galicia. It failed miserably. The army was demoralized and, with so many problems at home, it was uncommitted to any such battle. About forty thousand Russian soldiers deserted the battle.[6] Soon after, Russia deserted the war. The Russian people, again like their German neighbors, were impoverished and angry, with little hope for the future. As noted earlier, this is a bad emotional state from which to make any major, life-changing decisions. This is true for an individual or for a country.

At this time, Vladimir Lenin was the leader of the Marxist Bolsheviks, or Communist Party. His was just one of several political parties struggling for power in this chaos. Lenin offered the people what they wanted, adopting the slogan, "Bread, Peace, and Land." With that promise, support for the Bolsheviks grew rapidly in the cities and peasantry. On November 6, 1917, Lenin had enough support to send armed men (his "Red Guard") to surround a convention of soviet councils that had assembled from all over the country. The council was given no choice. With his coup complete, Lenin announced that the Bolshevik Council would lead the new Russian government.[7]

Only a minority of Russians actually wanted the Marxist Communists to take power. The provisional government had already set up elections a few weeks later, and the Bolsheviks received only about 25 percent of the vote. But it was too late. World War I was still being waged, and chaos reigned. In January 2018, Germany sent troops deep into Russia. With his troops in full retreat, Lenin had to agree to a peace treaty that gave up lands to Germany that were the home of fully a third of Russia's prewar population. In the end, Lenin had gathered enough support that the Communist Party became the ruling party of Russia. Though civil wars continued to break out as anti-Bolshevik factions battled the Red Army, they were to no avail. In 1922, Lenin proclaimed the formation of the Union of Soviet Socialist Republics (USSR), which would significantly change the course of world history.[8]

But the story does not end here. Lenin died in 1924, having replaced a monarchy with Communist rule. Unfortunately, like a kingship, Lenin's communist government did not spread its power to more than a handful of men. Lenin's successor was to be a man named Leon Trotsky, but a more brutal man named Joseph Stalin outmaneuvered Trotsky. Stalin was a ruthless dictator. In 1930, he ordered that all farms be made into state-run collectives. The displaced farmers and peasants, called "Kulaks," who objected to losing their lands, were imprisoned or sent to the frozen tundra of Siberia.[9] This campaign against the Kulaks rapidly evolved into one of the cruelest persecutions of the twentieth century.[10] Like Germany had campaigned against the Jews, Russia labeled the Kulaks as enemies of the state who should be blamed for the woes of their country. As a result of these policies, agricultural output plummeted, and the Russian people starved. Stalin joined with Adolf Hitler and Germany in 1939 to begin World War II. Only after Hitler turned against him and invaded Russia in 1941 did Stalin switch sides and fight with the Allied powers.

A Loss in Faith

Because they thought that God had permitted World War II, the Holocaust, and the Soviet rule of Russia, many Jews and Christians lost their faith in God and religion. The decisions of Adolf Hitler and the German people who supported him led to a tragic world war and the worst persecutions in the history of earth. The decisions of Vladimir Lenin, Joseph Stalin, and the Russian people in 1917 created an oppressive form of government in the largest country in the world. Many once-faithful citizens asked how a loving God could have allowed the depths of oppression, misery, and death that occurred from 1910 to 1945. But God did *not* make these decisions. The citizens of Germany and Russia had used their agency to choose leaders who led their nations into tragic outcomes.

The rule of earth that we must suffer the consequences for bad decisions of other people is hard to understand and accept. Couldn't God have just killed Hitler before he started his oppression of Jews and attack on Poland? In a continuation of that policy, couldn't God have also eliminated Genghis Khan, Joseph Stalin, John Wilkes Booth, and Lee Harvey Oswald before they accomplished their evil deeds? One can see how complicated Godly intervention could become. If God fixed our society's problems for us, it would be as if we had never left the premortal existence. So God has shown He will not interfere with our decisions, even if it leads to the death of millions.

The Cuban Missile Crisis in October 1962 took the world to the brink of worldwide nuclear war. Either John F. Kennedy of the United States or Nikita Khrushchev of Russia could have launched nuclear missiles at one another, but peace talks prevailed, and both countries backed away from war. I have heard speculation that God had a hand in these negotiations, but we have no proof. From past events, it appears more likely that God would have allowed us to destroy ourselves. If nuclear war had occurred, many more people would have blamed God and stopped believing in him. Few people appreciate the brutality of the rules that we must suffer for others' bad decisions. Unless we remain diligent in carefully selecting the wisest government leaders, our nations could again suffer as they have suffered before.

Due to our technology and population, we live in a day and age where you do not have to be a world leader to cause thousands of people to suffer for your decisions. On Sept. 11, 2001, a group of unstable, unremarkable men hijacked four large airliners. Two airliners were flown into the World Trade Center and one into the Pentagon. The decisions of these men horrified our nation and significantly afflicted untold thousands of lives. As we know, any civilized nation must have strong law enforcement to prevent evil men from afflicting innocent citizens. Yet law enforcement cannot always control those people who believe that justice lies in destruction and the deaths of innocents. Acts of terrorism will continue as we must continue to suffer the consequences of others' decisions.

In summary, the people around us—family, friends, strangers, and world leaders—can endanger our happiness and well-being. Agency has been granted to all of us, including a wayward child, an addicted friend, or a brutal world leader. No one can deny an adult the right to make self-destructive decisions, even when those decisions cause sorrow. Everyone must choose their own path to wisdom, and some pick hard paths indeed.

Chapter 11

Everyone Must Obey the Rules of Earth

As we all know from the Christmas story, when Joseph and Mary entered Bethlehem, they had to spend the night in a stable, because "there was no room for them in the inn" (Luke 2:7). One must wonder at the irony of that verse. The most important event in the history of the world occurred in a stable, which leads to the question, "Why didn't Heavenly Father just send a legion of angels to kick everyone out of the inn so Jesus's birth could have taken place indoors?" While we can admire the humility of such a birthplace, there is no indication in the scriptures that it was necessary for the Savior to be born in a barn. But without heavenly intervention, the earthly reality was that Joseph and Mary were not rich. They did not have the financial resources to outbid other residents in the inn and take their room. Heavenly Father did not send down angels to make it easier or more comfortable for Mary to give birth to His only begotten Son. Later, an angel appears to Joseph and instructs him to take his family into Egypt "for Herod will seek the young child to destroy him" (Matthew 2:13). Instead of forcing Joseph's family to go through the difficulties of a move, why didn't Heavenly Father just send that same task force of angels to kill Herod and eradicate the threat to the young Jesus? Wouldn't that have made it easier for everyone?

I propose that to qualify for a truly mortal ministry, the Savior had to strictly obey the rules of earth, just like everyone else. The Savior was not born into a rich or privileged family. He was born into poverty and undoubtedly had to help Joseph in extensive physical labor to provide for their family. Jesus had to suffer for the evil decisions of others—starting with having to move to Egypt to escape the crazed Herod. While on the cross, Jesus gave His Apostle John the responsibility of caring for Mary (John 19:27). So it appears likely that Joseph had died during the Savior's lifetime. Jesus also lost His favorite cousin, John the Baptist, when Herod Antipas beheaded him. So Jesus Christ also learned and grieved that temporal life is temporary with the losses from His own family.

Was the Earth a Place of Faith for the Savior?

During the accounts of the four Gospels, it is difficult to tell how much Jesus Christ knew about the future. He had spent his youth studying the Jewish religion as a foundation to His gospel understanding. He may have studied with John the Baptist. (Notice John's teachings in Matthew 3:2 are nearly exactly the same wording as Jesus's first teachings in Matthew 4:17.) Peter, James, and John were able to see the Savior converse with Moses and Elias, so there may have been other angelic instruction that we don't know about. Certainly we can expect that the Holy Ghost taught the Savior much of what He knew, but from one request the Savior made just before the Atonement, I don't believe the Savior knew everything about the earth life and His role in it.

As He knelt in the Garden of Gethsemane, the first thing the Savior said was, "O my Father, if it be possible, let this cup pass from me" (Matthew 26:39). Most readers will pass over this request and focus instead upon the Savior's next words of obedience: "Nevertheless not as I will, but as thou wilt." Yet, the initial request is by far the more revealing doctrine.

Any Primary child can tell you that the Savior absolutely *had* to pass through the Atonement. The entire plan of redemption revolved around the Atonement. It had to happen. Without the Atonement, our sins would keep us from returning to live with our Heavenly Father. As far as we know, our eternal progress would be halted. For years I contemplated why Jesus Christ would ask in the moments just before the Atonement if He could get out of it. I finally realized that only one answer made sense. Jesus was asking a question for the same reason anyone asks a question. He did not know the answer. Scriptures indicate that Jesus Christ did understand that He would go through an atonement, be crucified, and rise from the tomb in three days, but apparently He did not know if there were any other options to the plan. Mark's version of the Savior's request was, "Abba, Father, all things are possible unto thee; take away this cup from me" (Mark 14:36). The Savior was mistaken in His premise that God the Father could remove the need for Him to pass through the Atonement. The plan of salvation and redemption both depended on the Savior carrying out the Atonement at this time and place. As mentioned earlier, it was the responsibility of God the Father to make sure the plan went forward.

On a side note, it makes me feel closer to the Savior to know that He also had to live by faith. If I knew everything that was going to happen, life would not be as challenging, because I could prepare for it all. Jesus had to know a lot. Obviously He had to establish His new doctrine and be aware of the deadline that loomed before Him, so it appears that He understood the general path of His earthly ministry and the main reason He was on the earth. But it appears that Jesus had to have faith regarding some very important details of His life. Even the Savior had to live in a world of uncertainty and hope.

Consequences of the Savior's Choice of Time and Place

The Savior came to earth during the reign of the Roman Empire. Scriptures tell us that the Savior would come to earth in "the meridian of time" (Moses 6:62; D&C 39:3). However, there is really no explanation in the scriptures as to why Jesus needed to make His earthly appearance when He did. In *Jesus the Christ*, James E. Talmage explains,

> The advent of the Savior's advent was preappointed . . . The long history of the Israelitish nation had unfolded a succession of events that found a relative culmination in the earthly mission of the Messiah.[1]
>
> The religion of the time was a matter of ceremony and formality, of ritual and performance; it had lost the very spirit of worship, and the true conception of the relationship between Israel and Israel's God was but a dream of the past.[2]

Jesus Christ was born for several important reasons besides just carrying out the Atonement. By the time of the Savior's birth, all spiritual aspects of the religion of the Jews of the Holy Land had been lost. The time had arrived for mankind to do away with the Mosaic law and usher in the gospel of Jesus Christ. The Jews of the Holy Land were still God's chosen people, so it seems that the new doctrine had to be offered to them first. The Savior established new doctrine and commandments that were a significant departure from the Mosaic Law. He petitioned the children of Abraham to recognize Him as the Promised Savior and to accept His new gospel. To prove He was their Redeemer, Jesus Christ showed them miracles that exceeded anything done since the days of Moses. A few open-minded Jewish people did join the Church, But the Jewish leadership of Jerusalem—Sadducees, Pharisees, priests, and scribes—rejected the new religion to the point of conspiring to have the Savior killed. After that rejection, the gospel of "Christ crucified" (1 Corinthians 1:22) could then be preached to the Gentiles and the rest of the world.

Because His mission was to preach to the Jewish people, the Savior was born in Bethlehem around the year AD 0 (more probably 3 BC). Since Jesus Christ had to obey the rules of earth, there were severe consequences to this choice of time and place. Earth life was not easy at that time. There was no electricity, air-conditioning, indoor plumbing, or other luxuries of our modern life. In depictions of the Savior, He usually appears in a white, spotless robe. In reality, the Savior lived in a hot and dusty landscape, and He probably walked wherever He went. His robes were much more likely to have been continually stained with layers of dirt and sweat. Except for the Atonement, there are no indications that the Savior ever had help from angels or priesthood power to make His life easier. The Savior endured the difficulties of ancient life that we only read about. To see how dedicated Heavenly Father and Jesus Christ really were to everyone obeying the rules of earth, we have to go to the end of the Savior's mortal life.

During the time and place of the Savior's life, His homeland was under the political authority of the Roman Empire. At the height of its glory, the Roman Empire stretched from the North Atlantic to the Persian Gulf, a vast territory. The Romans brought order and civilization to these lands, but they did so by conquering, occupying, and taxing each nation. Administering the collection of those taxes, road construction, and provision of supplies to the military was a huge challenge for Rome. Local uprisings and revolutions interfered with their well-organized operations. Roman troops would be sent in to quell the militants, but it was an expensive endeavor that pulled their armies away from further expanding the Empire.

Rome wanted their conquered nations to fear them, remain peaceful, and continue paying their taxes. So Roman leaders did all they could to intimidate and subdue their subjects. Revolts were not tolerated, and revolutionaries were severely punished, almost always with death by crucifixion. It is believed that Rome adopted crucifixion from the Carthaginians, but Rome perfected the process as a form of capital punishment. The Romans were as logical as they were brutal. Crucifixion sent exactly the message they wanted to communicate to their subjects.

Crucifixion has always been recognized as one of the most painful forms of execution. Those who fought against Rome knew an agonizing death awaited them if they were captured alive. Crucifixions were held in public areas, often just outside city walls or along major roads. During crucifixions, onlookers could see what pain awaited them should they decide to defy Rome. Often bodies would be left on their crosses for days afterward, functioning as brutal reminders to passing residents and travelers. The crucifixion message was clear. Don't mess with Rome.

Most Christians are only aware of the crucifixion of the Savior and two robbers, but Rome actually crucified tens of thousands of people. Captured enemy soldiers, criminals, rebels, and Roman army deserters were punished by crucifixion. In 76 BC, a slave named Spartacus led a rebellion against his Roman masters. Spartacus gathered 100,000 slaves and, after several victories, marched toward Gaul and then Rome. But Spartacus was defeated in the battle of Silarius by the Roman General Marcus Licinius Crassus. Crassus ordered the crucifixion of 6600 rebels, posting one cross every hundred feet for sixty miles on the road to Rome.[3]

By being born in the Roman Empire as the Lamb of God, the Savior essentially chose the method of His execution. It must have been a hard choice indeed. The intent of this chapter is to communicate the importance of the rules of earth to God the Father and Jesus Christ. There was no cheating the requirements of earth life, even for the only begotten Son of God.

The Process of Crucifixion

Many of the rules of crucifixion were established by Roman law and had to be followed precisely. Crucifixion was actually a process that lasted for several hours. Once a guilty verdict was handed down on a prisoner, the process began. Scourging or flogging was the legal preliminary to almost every crucifixion.[4] This was done with a short whip called a flagrum, which was usually equipped with not just one, but several leather thongs. Each thong had iron balls or bone fragments tied along its length. The victim was stripped of his clothing and his hands were tied to an upright post. The Roman soldier would then swing the whip in a circular pattern, ending with the whip ends digging into the back of the man being scourged. The iron balls would cause extensive bruising; the thongs and bone fragments would cut through skin and muscle. The executioner would flog one side of the back, switch positions, and attack the other side. This pattern of abuse left parallel bloody stripes along the back, angling diagonally down from the victim's shoulders across his back. The stripes laid onto the back of the Savior are referred to in several scriptures (Isaiah 53:5; 1 Peter 2:24; Mosiah 14:5). Such floggings were intended to weaken the convict to a state just short of collapse or death. By Jewish law, a maximum of thirty-nine lashes could be applied to a victim. The Romans did not have a maximum. We don't know how many lashes the Savior received.

Even though the imprisonment, trial, and scourging took place inside the city, the execution had to be moved to a place outside of the city's walls. Thus, the convict was laid on his back with his head resting on the beam of wood that would become the horizontal crosspiece of his cross. The victim's arms were tied to this crosspiece so it rested on his shoulders. The condemned carried the heavy wood through the busy streets and out of the city. The upright posts on which the crosspieces would be mounted were already set in the ground and waiting at the site of the crucifixion. Jesus is often depicted as having to carry the whole cross through the streets of Jerusalem, but this is almost surely incorrect.[5] Between the suffering of the Atonement the evening before, a night of being shuttled from one trial to another, and the scourging, Jesus was certainly at the point of collapse. He could not bear the weight of carrying his crossbar. The guards, seeing this, forced a man named Simon of Cyrene to carry it for him.

Upon arrival at the site of execution, the victim was legally allowed to drink wine mixed with myrrh or gall. Gall acted as an analgesic to reduce the pain of the scourging and crucifixion. It was the only bit of mercy afforded by the Romans, but for this execution, the wine given to the Savior had spoiled and turned into a bitter vinegar. After tasting it, Jesus refused to drink more (Matthew 27:34).

The convict was then nailed to the cross. Since the palms of the hands could not withstand the weight of the body, nails were driven through the wrists. The body and crossbar were then lifted up onto the post and the crosspiece affixed with ropes or nails. The feet were then nailed to the upright post, with one nail driven into each foot. This required that the knees be considerably bent to align the feet and the post, though depictions of the Savior on the cross do not usually make it appear so.

A sign was then posted above the crucified man's head, identifying the victim's name and his crime. Once again, the Romans wanted to be clear about their laws and the punishment one could expect for breaking them. In Jesus's case, Pilate himself wrote the title sign JESUS OF NAZARETH THE KING OF THE JEWS in Hebrew, Greek, and Latin (John 19:19–20).

It was customary for the soldiers on duty to divide the clothes of the victim between themselves. In the case of Jesus's execution, rather than tearing the coat into four pieces and greatly reducing its value, the soldiers agreed to gamble for it. It was also customary that, if death was taking too long to occur, the Roman soldiers could break the leg bones of the crucified. The shock of this assault would either cause immediate death or, since the crucified could no longer use his legs to take pressure off his arms and lungs, hasten the suffocation. This the Roman executioners did to the two thieves crucified with Him. In finding Jesus Christ was already dead, the soldiers did not bother to break His legs.

Last, by Roman law, the family of the executed man could then take the body for burial after obtaining permission from a Roman judge. Thus, Joseph of Arimathaea "besought Pilate that he might take away the body of Jesus: and Pilate gave him leave" (John 19:38). The Roman soldiers would have been in serious trouble if they had released an executed man who was still living to his family. So, for certainty's sake, a guard would often stab the body with a sword or spear to create a mortal wound and assure the death of the crucified. Just before His body was taken down and released to His family and friends, the Savior was stabbed for this very purpose, thus creating the wound in his side. In summary, many people believe that the crucifixion of Jesus Christ was somehow special, or especially designed for Him, but the crucifixion of the Savior was in no way special. The Roman soldiers chosen for the task followed the same set procedure for crucifixion that they had followed hundreds of times before.

Each step of the Savior's life depended on meeting requirements set forth for Him in the premortal existence. It was the responsibility of the Savior to take His gospel to the remnant of the children of Abraham in ancient Israel, thus He was born in a specific place and time. But the Jews rejected His message, betrayed Him, and demanded his execution. The Atonement was a task given specifically to the Savior Jesus Christ, a task foreseen by Old Testament prophets, which was sealed by His death. Finally, the crucifixion was the result of the time and place in which the Savior had to come to deliver His message to the Jewish people. In order to meet the requirements of the eternal laws of justice and mercy, the Savior had to die for our sins. To meet the requirements of the rules of earth, the Savior had to play the hand He was dealt, born in poverty and dying by crucifixion.

Other Famous Deaths That Obeyed the Rules of Earth

We know from our history books that the Prophet Joseph Smith died from being shot by a mob in Liberty, Missouri, on June 27, 1844. Abraham Lincoln died twenty years later from being shot by an assassin at the Ford Theatre in Washington, DC. Mahatma Ghandi, Martin Luther King, President John F. Kennedy, and other world leaders met the same fates. Being shot by an assassin is neither a glorious nor a noble way to die. One might think that the great deeds of great men might earn them protection from the rule that we must suffer for the evil decisions of others, but no such reprieve is allowed. Evil men, who disagreed with the beliefs of these national leaders enough to spill blood on their hands, killed them by assassination. We mourn the loss of great leaders, for they are so hard to find. Some even curse God for allowing the lives of good rulers to be taken, but the rules of earth must be followed by all, including our finest leaders. There are no exceptions, a fact we should consider as we bemoan the trials in our own lives.

Throughout history, the world has needed God to interfere numerous times to prevent wholesale misery and death. But misery and death are not the worst things that could happen on earth. The loss of earth as a testing place, thus destroying the very intent of its creation, would be worse. If God had stepped in and fixed the world's tragedies, mankind would never have had to overcome disease. God would have simply handed us the knowledge. Men and women would have never learned the horrors of war if God had stepped in and prevented them. Since God did not fix these challenges of life, each rule has caused much suffering and death—all in the effort to teach men and women the consequences of their decisions. Once enumerated, the rules of earth are obvious. These are the realities of life, and we see their consequences on a daily basis. The rules are harsh. It is often hard to see past those hardships to realize the rules are necessary for this earth life to be the learning and proving ground that it is.

Chapter 12

Prayer: Asking for Exceptions to the Rules

IN THE COURSE OF READING THIS BOOK, you may be feeling that you should restrict the blessings you request due to the rules of earth. You may even wonder if it's worth it to pray, since God is so limited by His own laws and restrictions. The goal of this book is certainly not to discourage your prayers. God has been managing His restrictions for thousands of years, so you don't have to worry whether your requests are out of bounds. Nonetheless, simply understanding God's plan and its requirements may help manage your expectations.

In offering your prayers, it also helps to understand in what you place your faith. Many people think that to have faith, you need only believe in God's *existence*. The real challenge in having faith when you ask for blessings is to believe that everything *will turn out well in the end*. We understand that mortal life is a long road, filled with potholes and rough spots. Believing that God is with us on the journey is a long-term type of faith, but it is the kind of faith that endures. As Howard W. Hunter put it,

> If prayer is only a spasmodic cry at the time of crisis, then it is utterly selfish, and we come to think of God as a repairman or a service agency to help us only in our emergencies.[1]

So, when you pray, make it a long-term commitment, and be assured you can ask God for whatever you want. He will sort through your requests and decide how best to answer your prayers and give you your needed blessings. God is your partner in getting you and your family through this earth life as unscathed as possible. Understanding the challenges God has in fulfilling His role will only make you a better and wiser partner. Prayer is an important aspect of that partnership, a communication we need to consider next.

THE AUDACITY OF PRAYER

The dictionary defines a miracle as "an extraordinary event manifesting divine intervention in human affairs."[2] Given that definition, can you think of any blessing that is not a "divine intervention in human affairs?" In any prayer, you are asking for at least one miracle, probably more. If we weren't so accustomed to asking for blessings daily, the sheer audacity of asking God for a miracle that circumvents His rules of earth would be shocking. It is a bit like a young basketball player approaching the head referee to ask to be allowed to run with the ball, step out of bounds, and push people aside when he drives to the basket.

"No," the referee responds, "those rules are in place for a reason."

"But," the players explains, "I need exceptions to the rules just for me and just this one game. Please!"

"No," the referee patiently answers. "If I let you run with the ball, you will never learn to dribble. If I let you step out of bounds, you will never learn discipline. If I let you push people aside, you will never learn how to compete fairly with the other team. Then the other players on both teams will notice you are getting special attention, and the whole game will fall apart."

"But Dad . . ."

Most of the time, like a referee, God must remain neutral when calling a game. Most of the time, God must set aside any favoritism and insist that everyone play by the same rules. Granted, real life is not a basketball game, but asking for an exception to the normal rules of earth is asking God to deliver a miracle to you. Those miracles must not threaten the faith basis of earth life nor suspend laws of physics. They must be explicable by natural processes. There are requirements of what a miracle can be. You should probably realize this as you kneel by your bed tonight and ask God for more exceptions to His rules.

Prayer—and What You Are Actually Requesting

Many churches have rote prayers that are offered as a form of worship. Many Christians recite the Lord's Prayer (Matthew 6:9), which gives thanks and asks for general blessings. Even outside of those word-for-word repetitions, many personal prayers have a standard format. Most of us start out by thanking God for blessings. Appreciation is both deserved and expected by the Lord. We don't want our Heavenly Father to think that we do not appreciate our blessings of family and good health (D&C 59:21). The appreciation should be sincere and not simply a strategy to receive more blessings from God. This is not as obvious or as simple as one might think. When we approach God in prayer in the middle of a crisis, one purpose consumes our thoughts. Recounting and appreciating past blessings calms us down and helps put the present disruptions of our lives into context. Only then should we ask for the next solution to our problems.

I don't know about your personal prayers, but the blessings I typically request of God are admittedly consistent. I choose the wording of my prayers so that it doesn't sound like I am asking for great miracles, but if you translate what I am asking behind those carefully worded prayers, you will see that I am asking for some serious heavenly intervention. The wording of my prayers and, to be very honest, *what I am actually asking the Lord to do* goes something like this:

I ask that Thou would bless my family and me with safety in our travels. (*What I am really saying is that if we are about to get into an auto accident, please step in and divert the car that is going to crash into us.*)

Please bless me with good health. (*Or, despite my advancing age, lack of exercise, and occasionally poor diet, please adjust my physical body to not get sick or injured.*)

I ask that Thou would bless my children to be wise and make good decisions. (*If any of my children are heading toward a risky financial decision, a poor marital decision, or any decision that will bring them pain, please influence them to reconsider and prevent them from this poor choice. Actually, because I love them dearly and hate to see them in pain, don't let them make any mistakes. In fact, just take away their agency to make bad decisions entirely . . .*)

The last request may be a bit of an exaggeration—but not by much. When I ask God to bless my daughter in her travels, I am asking Him to influence her and the drivers around her to not divert their attention from safe driving. But even if my daughter is texting on her phone and blows through a red light, my prayer is that she doesn't have to suffer the consequences of her bad decision. God, please protect her, no matter what.

I fully realize that this book has argued that earth life was designed for us to gain wisdom by learning from the consequences of bad decisions. Like you, I know all this, but I still pray that my loved ones will not have to suffer from their mistakes. We might be willing to let a toddler tumble to the carpeted floor as he learns to walk. There is, after all, no lasting damage. But if a teenage daughter is distracted in her driving and is about to be involved in a serious car crash, we want God to interfere. We are willing to trade every blessing we are due from our righteous living so that our children do not have to suffer terrible consequences for their unwise decisions. For serious issues like this, we don't care one whit about the rules of earth or that we should learn to deal with all the consequences of our decisions. We don't care that this needs to be a world of faith and God cannot publicly demonstrate His power. We do not hesitate to ask God to ignore the rules completely and bless our child with a miracle immediately when one is needed.

I am not criticizing this attitude. I recognize it in myself in every prayer I offer. I love my children a lot more than I love the rules of earth. Preserving the rules of earth is not my job, but maintaining those Rules *is* our Heavenly Father and Jesus Christ's responsibility. We should probably try to understand their perspective and the difficult position we put God in as we pray for Him to bypass those rules. But it is not the goal of this chapter or book to ever discourage prayers of faith. Prayer is our opportunity to consult with our Heavenly Father. You should have faith that God will help you resolve the problems in your life, knowing that the solution may not come as immediately, completely, or as effortlessly as you might wish.

Exceptions to the Rules

The Savior gave a great lesson about making exceptions to rules—and it all started with a few hungry disciples. As Jesus and His followers walked through a wheat field, a few of them stripped some kernels off their stalks. They removed the chaff by rubbing the wheat between their hands. They threw the kernels into their mouths to soften, chew, and consume. Technically, this simple act was breaking the law of the Sabbath. The disciples were both harvesting wheat and threshing it, which was work forbidden in the Ten Commandments (Exodus 20:10) and elsewhere (Exodus 34:21). When the Pharisees saw this, they immediately addressed the Savior.

> At that time Jesus went on the sabbath day through the corn; and his disciples were an hungred, and began to pluck the ears of corn, and to eat. But when the Pharisees saw it, they said unto him, Behold, thy disciples do that which is not lawful to do upon the sabbath day. (Matthew 12:1–2)

Jesus makes no effort to argue that His disciples were just grabbing a snack in a way that could hardly be considered work. By strict Jewish law, the Savior recognized that His disciples were breaking a rule. Instead, Christ begins His argument with a story from the Old Testament in which King David also broke a law associated with eating.

> But he said unto them, Have ye not read what David did, when he was an hungred, and they that were with him; How he entered into the house of God, and did eat the shewbread, which was not lawful for him to eat, neither for them which were with him, but only for the priests? (Matthew 12:3–4)

Jesus is referring here to the account in 1 Samuel 26, when David and his men were fleeing from one of the murderous rampages of King Saul. The party was about three days into their flight when they stopped at the home of the priest Ahimelech for a short rest. David and his men were hungry after their journey and needed food. However, the only bread Ahimelech had available was shewbread, an unleavened bread hallowed for priest consumption only (Leviticus 24:9). So David and Ahimelech made an exception to the rule, and David and his men ate the shewbread. David's need was greater than the need to follow a ritual law of who could eat a special bread. Since the Lord had anointed David to become the king of Israel, it was a good bet that He approved the exception.

The Savior continues to elaborate His lesson by pointing out yet another exception to the rule of working on the Sabbath day.

Or have ye not read in the law, how that on the sabbath days the priests in the temple profane the sabbath, and are blameless? (Matthew 12:5).

By Jewish law, each Sabbath day, two lambs, flour mingled with oil, and drink were given in a burnt offering to the Lord (Numbers 28:9–10). This offering was considered a temple ordinance within Jewish law. However, the preparation of that burnt offering actually violated rules of food preparation on the Sabbath. Since a burnt offering temple ordinance superseded Sabbath day observance, the priests doing the work were held blameless. The daily temple ordinance was the higher commandment. With these two examples, Jesus demonstrated to the Pharisees that the laws of God sometimes conflict. When that happens, one needs to determine the higher law and follow it. For example, attending church on Sunday is part of the commandment to honor the Sabbath day, but if you are sick with the flu, the higher law is not to infect fellow members of your congregation with your virus. You are excused from attending church. (Thus, if you are sick, please follow the higher commandment and stay home!)

The Savior continued with His lesson. Completion of temple ordinances was of greater import than the rules that forbid preparing a meal on the Sabbath, but even more important than the temple ordinances was the will of the Savior, as He makes clear in the next verses.

> But I say unto you, That in this place is one greater than the temple. But if ye had known what this meaneth, I will have mercy, and not sacrifice, ye would not have condemned the guiltless. For the Son of man is Lord even of the sabbath day. (Matthew 12:6–8)

The Savior's decision not to rebuke His men established the highest law. Jesus made His decision knowing that His followers were hungry. Gathering small handfuls of wheat, rubbing it between their palms, and eating it was a small thing. The commandment to honor the Sabbath day is meant to demonstrate sacrifice of our normal day-to-day routine, but in this case, the Savior decided that mercy was more important than sacrifice. Since He was the Savior, Jesus was also the Lord of those Sabbath rules, so He had the authority to overrule them. The Savior had made His point and could have concluded His lesson at this point, but just two verses later, He taught the principle to the Pharisees yet again.

> And when he was departed thence, he went into their synagogue: And, behold, there was a man which had his hand withered. And they asked him,

> saying, Is it lawful to heal on the sabbath days? that they might accuse him. (Matthew 12:9–10)

Since the Pharisees had just heard this lesson, they already knew the answer to their question. It is interesting to note that the Pharisees did not ask, "Can you heal that hand, Jesus?" They appeared to accept that Jesus could heal the hand but queried if the Sabbath was the right day to do it. One has to wonder why the Pharisees wished to accuse the Savior, all the while knowing He had godly powers. No wonder the Savior called them blind (Matthew 15:14). In any case, since there was no specific rule in Jewish law to prevent one from doing miracles on the Sabbath, this was a rhetorical question designed to entrap the Savior.

> And he said unto them, What man shall there be among you, that shall have one sheep, and if it fall into a pit on the sabbath day, will he not lay hold on it, and lift it out? How much then is a man better than a sheep? Wherefore it is lawful to do well on the sabbath days. Then saith he to the man, Stretch forth thine hand. And he stretched it forth; and it was restored whole, like as the other. (Matthew 12:11–13)

The Savior reinforced the higher law principle He had just explained. He chose to work on the Sabbath day and heal the crippled man's hand. Just as we have a moral obligation to show mercy to a stranded sheep on the Sabbath, one must show mercy to an ailing person as well. Thus, in this New Testament teaching, we see the principle behind making exceptions to the rules of God—or the rules of earth in this case. If you pray for a miracle, God will judge your petition as He judges all prayers. Can this request be granted without breaking a rule of earth? It would help God out immensely if you would structure your requests so that He can more easily grant your petition. Thus, you may want to consider the following restrictions that have governed miracles for thousands of years.

Miracles Must Have a Natural Explanation

Throughout this book, the principle that Earth must remain a place of faith has been mentioned numerous times. This is an important rule that cannot be broken (well, until the Second Coming, when the rules all change). As discussed, for the earth to remain a place of faith, there can be no documentable, unexplained miracles. So, the first guideline I would suggest in asking blessings in prayer is *do not ask for a miracle for which there can be no natural explanation.*

In helping the Mormon pioneers cross the plains, God may have had been able to provide them with a fleet of modern-day, air-conditioned Jeep Cherokees. Such a miracle would have made the trek much easier for this faithful group of Latter-day Saints. But there could have been no natural explanation for such a miracle. How would faith in God and the Church be affected if Church history museums could display sport utility vehicles used by the Saints in 1847 to migrate to the West? Admittedly, this is an extreme and fictitious example, but if we look at past miracles, we see that each one can be explained by natural causes. For example, many consider the arrival of seagulls to consume hordes of crickets (or katydids) that were devouring the crops of the early Saints in 1848 a miracle. But the event still has a natural explanation. A number of other miracles are reported in journals of other early Saints. You may be convinced that these reported miracles were truly heaven-sent, but each has a natural explanation as well.

The Miracles of Jesus Christ

With the declaration that miracles must have natural explanations, the argument can be made that Jesus Christ did many miracles that did not have natural explanations. Indeed He did. Christ's miracles were inexplicable. This was, in fact, their main purpose.

Many Christians believe that Jesus did miracles to heal people, which is partially true. The miracles of Jesus did help a few people. He helped the blind to see and the lame to walk, both in the Holy Land and in Bountiful. But the number of blind He healed was a *very small* percentage of all the blind people who lived before, after, or in another location than Jesus during His ministry. It was miraculous that Jesus Christ healed the crippled man at the pool of Bethesda (John 5:2–9), but there have been millions of crippled people over the course of history that were not healed. There was a greater reason behind the Savior's healings. While it is wonderful that He could help those few people, the miracles of the Lord were accomplished to get the people to recognize His authority from God and come hear His message. In modern terms, miracles were a part of the Lord's marketing plan. When John the Baptist sent disciples to ask if

He was the long-awaited Savior, Jesus told them to tell John about His miracles as proof.

The blind receive their sight, and the lame walk, the lepers are cleansed, and the deaf hear, the dead are raised up, and the poor have the gospel preached to them. (Luke 7:22)

In John 9:2–3, just before He healed a blind man, Jesus revealed that the man was there and would be healed, "that the works of God should be made manifest in him." Jesus needed to show by miracles that He represented the works of God the Father.

If He had not used miracles to get people to come hear Him, Jesus would have spent three years knocking on doors to teach. Without miracles, He could never have spread His message far enough in such a short time to set the stage for the establishment of the Church. Miracles gave Jesus Christ legitimacy in His claims that He was the son of God.

But even these miracles meet the requirement that they could not be documentable proof that God lives. Jesus was talking to mostly poor and uneducated people in the Holy Lands over two thousand years ago. There was no way to properly document His miracles. It is interesting that Christ never sought an audience with Herod or Pilate to show them miracles that could have been documented by the court. In any case, the miracles done by Jesus Christ Himself were accomplished in a very specific time and place. They really should not be used as examples in discussions of the dictates imposed upon present-day miracles.

Medical Miracles

When discussing miracles in Sunday classes, medical miracles are probably the most commonly cited. A newborn baby that has been struggling to breathe suddenly stabilizes. A teenager in a coma from a car rollover regains consciousness after two days of ward prayer and fasting. The father of a young family has a heart attack but recovers miraculously to the astonishment of his doctors. There is a good reason for the abundance of miracles that occur in hospitals. If you think about it, medical miracles are the easiest for the Lord to arrange. The human body has a great capacity for recuperation after traumatic events such as birth, injury, or disease. The natural explanation for a medical miracle is simply, "He got better."

Especially with advances in our medical technology, God can work His miracles secretly, drawing little unwanted attention.

But one must understand the limitations under which God must work. God can nudge a medical condition, but He does not bless His children beyond the medical technology of the time. A good example of this principle may be found in statistics on infant mortality. In 1900, for every one thousand live births, approximately one hundred infants (or 10 percent) died before age one year.[3] Since 1900, improved maternal nutrition, the use of antimicrobial agents in birthing, safer blood transfusions, and milk pasteurization contributed to a sharp decline in infant mortality. By 1997, the infant mortality rate had declined to 7.2 per one thousand (or 0.72 percent) live births. However, we cannot imagine that family prayers changed over that century. Couples who had a baby born and get sick in 1900 would have prayed to their Heavenly Father to heal their child with the same earnestness and fervor that parents pray for their sick children today. But in 1900, medical knowledge was not nearly as advanced as it is today. Despite an equal number of heartfelt prayers by her family, a baby girl born in earlier days was fourteen times more likely to die in infancy as her distant cousin born in 2018. Even medical miracles have their limits. If you are asking that your ninety-five-year-old grandmother recover from her arthritis, you will probably be disappointed. There is no cure for arthritis,[4] and there would be no natural explanation for your grandmother's recovery.

One last aspect of medical miracles should be discussed. In today's medical community, patients and their families have been given more decision-making power in their treatments. For example, if your elderly father is on life support and doctors are advising it be discontinued, you have difficult choices to make. Your father's doctors will try to explain to you the results of blood tests, x-rays, and other exams. Hospital administrators will explain insurance coverage, copayments, and other economic realities of continued treatment. In making such difficult decisions, one should not, even in the secret corners of your mind, factor in the possibility of a medical miracle. Desperation often leads to grasping at any positive outcome. Sometimes desperate Christians will think that demonstrating faith means one must deny reality. All of the scriptural verses on faith (Alma 32:21, 30, 41) refer to having faith in God's existence, the Atonement, and the gospel, nothing doubting. But these verses do not encourage you to have faith that God is going to do exactly what you want Him to do. It is actually a bit presumptuous and sometimes dangerous to assume, or "have faith," that God is going to come through with a miracle. One of the saddest stories in Church history occurred when the Willie and Martin handcart companies had "faith" that God would delay the winter snowstorms to allow them to reach Zion. These faithful but mistaken Saints left Florence, Nebraska, in Oct. 1847. The snows fell, and these pioneers endured weeks of severe hunger, cold, exhaustion, and the deaths of loved ones—all because of a misunderstanding of the principle of faith.

While we should always pray for what we need, we should not base our decisions in life on the expectation that miracles will occur. Such is not faith. God wants you to accept the realities of your situation, whether they are medical or financial. We need to come up with our own solutions. Nonetheless, I have seen faithful Saints refuse to deal with pressing decisions because they felt it would demonstrate a lack of faith that God would resolve the issues for them. We are to have faith in God, not in the miracles you want Him to perform. Don't go into deep credit card debt, having faith that God will bless you to win the lottery to pay it off.

The Nephites had faith in God, but they still mobilized their armies when attacked by the Lamanites. Our pioneer ancestors had faith in God but still abandoned their homes as the mobs advanced. Joseph Smith and Hyrum Smith died at a time when the loss of leadership threatened the very existence of the church. In these times, one might have thought that the Church's extreme need coupled with the faith of all of its members would have essentially guaranteed the granting of a miracle, but miracles did not occur in those worst of times, demonstrating the danger of expecting specific miracles in a specific time and place.

The most knowledgeable people to help you make decisions about your critically ill father are his doctors. They will not factor in the likelihood of a miracle into their recommendations. Nor should they. Doctors need to keep both feet planted in the natural world when it comes to these decisions—and so must we.

Miracles in Public Settings

The second guideline you might consider in asking for blessings is to *never ask for any miracle to occur in a public setting.* As just described, miracles must have natural explanations. This is much more difficult to do if the miracle is both inexplicable and has multiple witnesses to testify it occurred. Thus, angels cannot stop a speeding car from crashing into a crowd of innocent people. Gunmen have never been struck down while shooting people from the top of a building. Suicide bombers cannot be levitated out of a crowd just before the explosion. Crippled people are not really healed by televangelists on national television. It is simply against the rule that the earth must remain a place of faith.

Miracles in Competitions

Whether it is an action-packed athletic event, a musical competition, the state finals in debate, or a chess match, competition drives us to be better in our chosen field. But rules of fair play are paramount in such competition. What is the goal of a football game? Besides entertaining spectators, athletic events are played to determine which team is better at playing football. They are not played to see which team can get more heavenly help from God to win the game. However, we hear the word "miracle" used a lot in sports. When the United States hockey team unexpectedly beat the Soviet Union in the first medal round of the 1980 Winter Olympics, it became known as the "Miracle on Ice." Since the Soviet Union was our enemy in the undeclared Cold War at the time, it was easy for many Americans to believe that God had actually taken our side and helped us win.

No miracle in the sense of godly intervention occurred, because such intervention would have been cheating. God doesn't determine the most righteous team and send heavenly help. He doesn't have a favorite city, university, or nation that He supports more than others. If God was to help one football team over another in a game, how would we know which was actually the better football team in the end? When the Brigham Young University football team plays Notre Dame or Southern Methodist, should God help the school affiliated with the religion He prefers? This cannot be, of course. If God ever makes His preference in religion known, it will not be through a football game. We should be careful in our prayers before competitions. We may pray that our team can do its best and not be injured, but we should probably not ask God to bless one team to win over another.

Overriding Agency

The next guideline in asking for blessings in prayer is to *never ask the Lord to override the agency of one of His children.* On one hand, this seems obvious. Agency is an important right of earth life. The War in Heaven was fought over this very principle, so any petition to take it away from someone will probably not be granted. On the other hand . . . let's face it—loved ones can do foolish things with their lives. I have found myself praying so hard that Heavenly Father persuade, prompt, influence, and "soften hearts" that I realize my intent has somewhat accidentally gone from loving prayer to a request for whatever strong-arm tactics He can use. My well-intentioned prayer has become a plea for God to steer family or friends (over which I have no control) in the right direction. I can't imagine that I am the only person to have ever done this.

Praying for loved ones who seemingly move from one mistake to the next is frustrating. In the parable of the prodigal son, we can find hope for our own errant sons and daughters. We all know the setting of this parable. The prodigal son takes his inheritance and spends it all in riotous living. Finally, with his money spent and a famine in the land, the young man is forced to take a job feeding pigs. In desperation, the young man finally makes the transition for which his father had prayed. The first six words of the following verses are the most important.

> *And when he came to himself,* he said, How many hired servants of my father's have bread enough and to spare, and I perish with hunger! I will arise and go to my father, and will say unto him, Father, I have sinned against heaven, and before thee. (Luke 15:17–18; italics added)

The prodigal son "came to himself," looked at his life situation, and decided, "This is ridiculous. What am I doing here? My father's servants have more than enough food and I am starving. I'm going home!" What a marvelous piece of wisdom for such a foolish young man! Fortunately, his epiphany included the realization that he owed his father an apology immediately after their embrace.

One moral of this story is that sincere repentance of an errant son sometimes requires letting him hit rock bottom so he can recognize the need to change his life. *Wisdom must come before repentance.* The prodigal son had to "come to himself" and recognize how foolish he had been. Only then could his repentance be sincere. There is no evidence that God initiated the young man's recognition or repentance. Hunger and a desperate situation drove the prodigal son to recognize his unnecessary plight and take the steps needed to escape it. Likewise, Heavenly Father is waiting for in all His errant children to find wisdom and then repent. As earthly parents of such a child, you will almost certainly have to wait patiently as well. Rarely do promptings, bribes, or threats prompt wisdom. Usually earth life, with all its difficulties, must open the eyes of those who do not wish to see.

Praying for the World

Last, we come to the charitable act of praying for our country or the world as a whole. Praying for God to intercede in the affairs of the world is asking for a major miracle. But miracles first require faith. The Prophet Spencer Kimball wrote an entire book on the subject in his aptly named book *Faith Precedes a Miracle.* President Kimball encouraged greater faith so that miracles could occur. His book was positive and optimistic. On the other side of the coin, the prophet Mormon witnessed the disappearance of miracles from the earth due to iniquity. Though he continued to pray for the Nephites, he realized that it would be to no avail. As faith diminishes, so do miracles. We can read of this progression in Mormon's account.

> But wickedness did prevail upon the face of the whole land, insomuch that the Lord did take away his beloved disciples, and the work of miracles and of healing did cease because of the iniquity of the people. (Mormon 1:13)
>
> Behold, I had led them, notwithstanding their wickedness I had led them many times to battle, and had loved them, according to the love of God which was in me, with all my heart; and my soul had been poured out in prayer unto my God all the day long for them; nevertheless, it was without faith, because of the hardness of their hearts. (Mormon 3:12)

Later, Mormon's son Moroni had to deal with the same increasingly wicked generation and also had to watch as miracles disappeared from the earth.

> And the reason why he ceaseth to do miracles among the children of men is because that they dwindle in unbelief, and depart from the right way, and know not the God in whom they should trust. (Mormon 9:20)

We have many other scriptural references that state that miracles cannot be wrought on a faithless or unrighteous generation (D&C 35:11; 3 Nephi 19:35; Moroni 7:37; Ether 12:12). When you pray for your country or the whole world, you are asking for blessings for a wide range of people, with varying levels of faith. A righteous generation, even with a few disbelievers, might still expect to receive blessings and miracles, but when the majority of a population has lost faith in God, it gets more difficult to expect such blessings.

The Pew Research Center conducted two Religious Landscape Studies, one in 2007 and another in 2014, to determine the level of religious observance in the U.S. In 2007, 39.5 percent of the U.S. population attended religious services on a weekly basis. By 2014, this number had dropped to 35.7 percent. Church attendance is predicted to continue its plummet. Of our oldest living generation, born between 1928 and 1945, 51 percent attend church weekly. Of the next generation, or Baby Boomers, 38 percent attend weekly. Finally, of the youngest adults, or Millennials, only 28 percent attend church on a weekly basis. Comparing daily prayer and importance of religion to these generations shows similar results. As the older generations pass away, it appears that church attendance will continue to fall off.[5]

Where does that put our population in regard to expecting blessings and miracles? It is hard to say or even venture a guess. But it does appear that the world is getting closer to the point where miracles will become less possible due to lack of faith and religious observance. This should not discourage our prayers, but we should realize that our world is not becoming wiser or more repentant, which makes blessings more difficult.

PRAYING FOR THE THIRD WORLD

At the time of this writing, the poor and dispossessed of the earth are not in a good place. Reportedly over 65 million displaced people have fled their homelands due to war, famine, and strife.[6] Governments and relief agencies are overwhelmed by the numbers of refugees. We see reports in the news every day. The despair may make our testimonies waiver as we wonder how God could allow so many people to suffer. Again, this is not

God's doing. I believe there is a plan for those dispossessed and poverty-stricken people. They will get their fair chance, though it may not be in this stage of our existence.

When considering the possible outcomes of Third World people, we should realize that earth life is only one act of a very long play. We don't even remember the first act of the play. Some think the premortal existence might have been the second act of the play, but we are not even sure of that. Earth life could be the third act. How many acts follow this one? In their criticisms of God's attention to the poor, many people seem to think there is only one more act after earth life, but though we know to expect a Final Judgment, we don't know for sure in which act that judgment will occur. Before we judge, we need to know the whole story.

Before Judging, Get the Whole Story

In my travels, the hardest airplane landing I have experienced was in Halifax, Nova Scotia. The jar of the landing hurt all the way down my back—and it made me mad. As we deplaned, I considered suggesting the pilot go back to flight school but contented myself with frowning disapprovingly at the airplane staff as I walked by. I retrieved my luggage, walked out of the terminal . . . and was nearly blown off my feet by hurricane-strength winds. I quickly retreated to the protection of the terminal. Having learned the whole story, the landing went from the worst landing of my life to the best. I considered going back to the plane to apologize to the pilot but didn't think security would let me through. Since then, I have sincerely thanked every pilot who has delivered me safely to my destination.

There are many examples in literature and movies about the dangers of making judgments before we have all the facts. Toward the end of William Shakespeare's love story *Romeo and Juliet*, Juliet takes a drug meant to make her appear dead so she doesn't have to marry another suitor. Her family concludes that she has committed suicide and puts her in the family crypt. Romeo never gets the message about the ruse. When he finds her in the tomb, Romeo assumes the worst. Not bothering to confirm the misdiagnosis, Romeo does not wait to get the whole story. In a tragic decision based on incomplete information, he drinks his own poison and dies.

Romantic comedies are rife with jealousies that arise from simple misunderstandings. In each storyline, love-struck characters cause havoc until the end of the movie, when they finally get the whole story. With so many examples of making poor judgments without getting all the facts, we should be more aware. We should recognize that we don't have the full story about our eternal life and what comes next. Millions of people have been born in Third-World countries with poor government, famine, disease, and poverty. For these people, it seems earth may have been a way station, where they received bodies, experienced life, and gained wisdom, but they never had the chance to learn the gospel and choose righteousness. I believe they will get other chances, though I don't have the full story about what their lives will be like when they do.

In the sciences, it is crucial to have all of the facts before making a conclusion. To those readers who are angry with God because of the state of the world—you need to delay your judgment until you have the whole story. We don't have nearly enough information to be angry with God. It will be when we have a full understanding of the whole story "when every nation, kindred, tongue, and people shall see eye to eye and shall confess before God that his judgments are just" (Mosiah 16:1). We just need to be patient until then.

Chapter 13

The Problem with Miracles

In the musical *Fiddler on the Roof*, Tevye, the father of a Jewish family living in Russia, gives permission for his daughter, Tzeitle, to marry a young tailor named Motel. Tevye had earlier promised Lazar Wolf, the town butcher, that he could marry Tzeitle, but Motel and Tzeitle's declaration of love and commitment convinces him to change his mind. Motel expresses his joy and disbelief at his good fortune by singing a song called "Miracle of Miracles." Motel refers to a number of Old Testament miracles before telling his fiancé, Tzeitle, in the last verse,

> But of all God's miracles large and small,
> the most miraculous one of all
> is the one I thought could never be—
> God has given you to me.

It is understandable for a newly engaged couple to be so in love that they think that God Himself miraculously arranged their meeting. Engagements happen every day, so other people might not consider them actual miracles.

The problem with miracles is that they must have a natural explanation, which makes it hard to positively identify them. Any such phenomenon can either be a miracle or a lucky coincidence. So it really depends on the nature and attitude of the person observing the phenomenon as to whether they believe they have seen a miracle. We are all biased in our judgments. Those who don't actively worship God *don't* want to admit that miracles occur. They have made the decision to ignore the spiritual side of their lives. They may not believe in God at all (atheists), or they may believe He is up there in Heaven but not involved with His children on earth (agnostics). For this group, possible miracles are discomforting news. Miracles would mean that God is real and actually involved in our earthly lives. Miracles would prove these groups were wrong in their decision to ignore the spiritual side of their lives—and people hate to be wrong. Since every miracle has a natural explanation, they will choose to accept only those natural explanations and continue their denial of God.

On the other hand, faithful believers in God are also biased. These people *want* to believe in miracles since a confirmation of supernatural powers would confirm their choices. By its nature, belief in God requires sacrifice. Active churchgoers spend much time and energy in church attendance, church callings, scripture study, and prayer. They sacrifice their money for tithing and other donations. After we dedicate our heart and soul to God, we *want* to find evidence that we are right. We want to find physical evidence of God, not just because we want to be proven correct in our choices, but also because we want the promise of eternal life to be real. If God is not real, then heaven is probably not real either. For faithful church members, this simply cannot be. Miracles confirm our belief in a loving Heavenly Father and our hope of an afterlife.

Within the group that recognizes miracles, there is still great diversity. Some people see miracles in every aspect of every-day life. How does one differentiate a miracle from a coincidence? The Catholic Church has a special division of authorities called the Miracle Commission. Their job is to travel to sites of proclaimed miracles and assess whether the church should accept the claim of a supernatural event. Unfortunately, no such committee evaluates the myriads of possible miracles we hear about each day, so we are on our own to decide if a miracle or a lucky coincidence has occurred—and we don't always agree in our conclusions.

T. C. Christensen wrote and directed the film *17 Miracles*. In a follow-up book, *More Than Miracles,* he explains that he has decided to never reveal the list of the seventeen miracles for which he named the film.

> I wanted to create discussion. The perception of miracles is a personal thing. What might be a miracle to one person might be just a coincidence to another. People have told me that they could count only five miracles in the film. Others have said they counted near thirty.[1]

In his book on miracles, Eric Metaxas states his agreement and observations.

> All of us have presuppositions about the nature of things, about whether something can be beyond what we experience with our five senses. Sometimes our presuppositions are the result of our education, but they are just as often determined by, or at least partly the result of, our upbringing and the culture in which we were raised. . . . One man's miracle is another man's eye-rolling *What's the big deal?* weird coincidence.[2]

So, does God send the fortunate outcomes in your life, or are those "miracles" just random, happy endings? On one hand, we are encouraged to seek for the hand of God in the good things that happen to us so we can better appreciate the world in which we live. But, on the other hand, we are also encouraged to seek out truth. So, to take a mere coincidence and call it a miracle is misleading and disingenuous.

THE DEFINITION OF A MIRACLE

As mentioned, a miracle is defined as "an extraordinary event manifesting *divine intervention* in human affairs."[3] But the definition of the word in our modern world has changed to "any event that turned out unexpectedly well." The word has been so overused that it is probably too late to save the definition.

It seems that people love to use the most extreme adjectives when describing an event to others, and "miracle" is one such adjective. So we have the Miracle on Ice and miracle comebacks in sports. If we run into a friend in a far country, we call it a miracle. We have miracles in song, miracle kitchen appliances, and miracles at Christmas. In one book with the word miracle in the title, the author defines a miracle as "a shift in perspective from fear to love."[4] While sweet, most shifting perspectives do not require divine intervention.

Changing the definition of the word miracle to include any unexpectedly fortunate event confuses the discussion. You don't know if the speaker is testifying that God has had a role in this incident or if she is just happy about something. To many faithful Christians, that distinction is important. If you are angry at God because everyone else seems to be seeing miracles besides you, be sure to check on their definition of what a miracle is.

TESTIMONIES AND FACEBOOK POSTS

Before proceeding with this discussion, we need to differentiate the personal recognition of a miracle from its publicly acclaimed recognition. If you personally believe that every good thing in your life is a miracle sent by God, you certainly may so believe. Miracles are exciting events, which can help you appreciate life and your Heavenly Father. If you believe you have witnessed a miracle in your life, you should certainly thank God in your prayers. Personally, I thank God for all the good things in my life. Please note that I don't really believe that God was the instigator of all of those good things. Most fortunate events are simply random good luck in being in the right place at the right time. I met my wife when I was ready to wed. My home came on the market when I was looking to buy, and so on. In reality, I don't care if God was or was not the source of those blessings. I appreciate the good things in my life anyway and thank Him for them whether He sent them or not. The Lord recognizes the value of appreciation in His children and encourages us to recognize His hand in our blessings (D&C 59:21). Personal recognition of blessings and prayers of appreciation are always appropriate, but if you want to publicly exclaim to the world that God blesses you with miracles, please do so carefully. You could be causing some good fellow Church members both grief and disillusionment.

Facebook, as everyone knows, is a major part of our social media platform today. Mark Zuckerburg launched the company in 2004, an event so significant that there is a movie about it. Originally, Facebook was marketed as a good way to stay in communication with friends, exchanging notes and photos about what was going on in our lives. With Facebook, losing touch with old friends need never happen again. In 2012, Facebook surpassed one billion active users. Today, almost 2.5 billion people log onto Facebook at least once a month. That is quite an audience.

For many users, Facebook changed from a pleasant way to keep in contact with friends to becoming a brag book. Seemingly innocent posts can go a long way in self-aggrandizement.

"Well, I just got back from the gym and my two-hour workout."

"We ate at the best five-star restaurant today!"

"Here are photos from our vacation in Tahiti. Wish you were here."

"I just posted photographs of our new home. The stained glass windows are awesome!"

Thus, you can use Facebook in one of two ways. You can use it as a means of staying in touch with friends and cheer them up with anecdotes and stories about your life, family, and foibles. Realizing that your posts can be taken as boastful, you are careful about what you write. You may even choose to not post some of the biggest "wins" in your life so your friends will not feel jealousy or discontentment with their own lives. On the other hand, Facebook can be used to covertly feed your ego by relating to everyone how awesome your life is. Social media is a great place for improving self-esteem.

Testimonies are much like Facebook posts in that your attitude determines their content. The point of a testimony is that it should lift up the people who hear it. Miracles are exciting. To think that God took His time to bless *you* with supernatural help or protection should be humbling. In bearing a testimony about a miracle that you believed happened to you, how are you going to relate the experience without communicating how special you think you are to the Lord? Simply put, there are contrasts in our lives that *need not* be emphasized in Church talks and testimonies. I pray that Church members more fully appreciate the difference between private recognition of God's blessings and their public declaration of miracles.

> Remember that that which cometh from above is sacred, and must be spoken with care, and by constraint of the Spirit; and in this there is no condemnation, and ye receive the Spirit through prayer; wherefore, without this there remaineth condemnation. (D&C 63:64)

Murphy's Law

The goal of this chapter is not to discourage the reader's personal testimony of modern-day miracles within the Church. They do occur. But we must realize that many people face ever-increasing hardships as one life challenge builds upon another—personal health issues, financial setbacks, marital problems, errant children, a poor work environment, depression, sleeplessness, etc. In that circumstance, miracles become hard to see. If you are in the middle of such life struggles, remember that the Lord has provided you with the miracle of the friends, neighbors, and Church members who are willing to help. These people can be the "miracle-workers" in your life if you let them. In the end, a faithful follower of God cannot make major blessings and miracles a requirement of continued faithfulness. There are rules as to when and how heaven-sent miracles can occur, and they must be followed.

For those who are angry with God because you are not receiving a much-needed miracle, please examine your expectations. I am a great believer in the adage called Murphy's Law—"Anything that can go wrong will go wrong." The logic behind Murphy's Law is simple. As you get into your car to drive to the airport, there is only one outcome that you will accept without complaint. You want to arrive at your gate safely and on time to catch your flight. But there are at least a hundred other outcomes that can occur. A car breakdown or accident, unexpected traffic delays, bad weather, full parking lots, or long airport security lines can cause you to miss your flight. If any of those disappointing outcomes occur, one could conclude that Murphy's Law is active in your life. On the other hand, if you successfully complete a business trip without any major delays, you should be delighted. Yes, sometimes life feels as if every day is an example of Murphy's Law, but minor miracles do happen, many of which you never see.

Chapter 14

Rule 7: The Church of Jesus Christ Must Be Staffed with Humans

THE SEVENTH RULE OF EARTH LIFE is that any church organized to worship God and Jesus Christ must be staffed by human beings. This means that the prophet, stake presidents, bishops, and Primary teachers must all be humans. There are absolutely no exceptions. This probably doesn't come as a surprise, but it has some serious ramifications. The Lord must choose men and women to serve in the Church, despite the fact that mankind has so many faults. Some our greatest thinkers have been the most critical of our species. Albert Einstein said, "Only two things are infinite, the universe and human stupidity, and I am not sure about the former." Mark Twain stated, "If you pick up a starving dog and make him prosperous he will not bite you. This is the principal difference between a dog and man." Jeffrey Holland was a bit kinder when he explained,

> So be kind regarding human frailty—your own as well as that of those who serve with you in a Church led by volunteer, mortal men and women. Except in the case of His only perfect Begotten Son, imperfect people are all God has ever had to work with. That must be terribly frustrating to Him, but He deals with it.[1]

I have talked to numerous people who were angry at God because they were first angry with their church. A leader in their ward, congregation, or stake has somehow offended them, and they have stopped attending church because of that offense. The logic of these people is that members of the Church of Jesus Christ should be more sensitive to giving offense. Because they are Church leaders, these men and women should be exceptionally humble, organized, educated in true doctrine, well-spoken, spiritual, and inspired. After all, such requirements are taught in the scriptures (Titus 1: 7–9).

With this presupposition, we should be able to look at religious history and encounter a string of good decisions and wise management. Instead, we find that the Lord allows the leaders of His Church to make poor decisions. The following review is not meant to be critical of those leaders. It is meant to demonstrate that Rule #7 has been in place for a long time.

THE ORIGINAL CHURCH OF JESUS CHRIST

After the Resurrection of Jesus Christ, the Apostles organized the Church as best they could. First, they called Matthias as a new apostle (Acts 1:26). The Savior appeared to Paul and called him to help in the work (Acts 9). Peter had his vision that the gospel should be preached to the Gentiles, which opened up a large new field of missionary work (Acts 10:34–35). The Church started growing rapidly.

But all was not well within the Church. Many Christians in Jerusalem, remembering his earlier oppressions, did not trust Paul. His life in danger, Paul fled to Tarsus to continue his missionary work, but Paul continued to cause dissonance. As missionaries, Paul and Barnabas argued so much that they agreed to go their separate ways (Acts 15:39). In Antioch, Paul publicly confronted the Prophet Peter about his treatment of the Gentiles (Galatians 2:11–14). Other problems surfaced. Travel was slow, so the Apostles often wrote letters to distant wards to encourage and teach doctrine. Church members who wanted to establish their own personal beliefs as Church doctrine started *forging* letters and signing them with the names of Apostles.[2]

Cultural diversity was high and problematic as Jewish, Gentile, Greek, and Roman converts brought some of their own beliefs and traditions into the Church with them. A major dispute arose as to whether new converts had to be circumcised. Paul and his Gentile converts thought it unnecessary. Church leaders and Jewish converts in Jerusalem believed it essential. In about AD 47, a major conference in Jerusalem failed to resolve the matter (Acts 11:27).[3] Paul's letters to new congregations in Rome, Corinth, Galatia, Colosse, Ephesus, and Thessaloniki repeatedly stressed the importance of avoiding false doctrine and dissension. As a member of the fledgling Church of Jesus Christ, one would have certainly wondered at the disorganization, conflicting teachings, and confusion within your congregation.

By the year AD 50, we have no more letters from Paul, Peter, or John. Around AD 60–70, it is believed that Peter and Paul were both executed in Rome. Legend has it that several of the other Apostles served missions in remote lands and died there. In any case, within a few decades, the leadership of the Church changed from that of the Savior's Apostles to that of bishops and other local leaders.

THE CATHOLIC CHURCH

The Church of Jesus Christ grew quickly and was so uniquely monotheistic that it started to clash with the Roman Empire. Christians would not participate in the worship of Roman gods, which was understandable, but they also refused to tone down their missionary efforts, which would have been politically advisable. Despite earlier instructions from Paul to submit to government authority and keep a low profile (Romans 13:1–3), charges were eventually laid against the Christians for disrupting the order of the state. During the second and third centuries, being Christian was a capital offense, and persecution steadily increased. Church leadership was unable to stem the abuse, and the very existence of the Church was threatened. Fortunately, in AD 312, Roman Emperor Constantine had a vision of Jesus Christ that changed the course of religious history. The Christian church was recognized as an officially sanctioned religion and the persecutions ceased.[4]

By this time, the Church had become known as the Catholic Church. While we believe many of the doctrines of the Church of Jesus Christ were lost over time, we must recognize that for over a thousand years the Catholic Church was the only recognized church of God for millions of Christians. The leadership of the Catholic Church became involved with the governments of Europe, sharing power with kings and heads of state. This was a dark time for Christian history. The Crusades began in 1095 and lasted into the sixteenth century, causing the deaths of millions of Muslims and Christians as the two religions fought for control of the Holy Land. The Spanish Inquisition, lasting from 1478–1834, was one of several brutal efforts by the church to remove heretics.[5] Religious tolerance hit an all-time low as Jews and Muslims were driven from their homes. In Great Britain, the Protestants and Catholic churches traded abuses, and the government supported whichever religion was practiced by the reigning monarch.[6] The hypocrisy of so much bloodshed in the name of the Christian church is obvious and hard to defend. Even today, in their attacks on religions, critics point out the violence afflicted on anyone who professed divergent beliefs in God. For two thousand years, countless church leaders, all of them flawed human beings, have made cruel and terrible choices.[7]

THE RESTORED CHURCH

In 1820, Joseph Smith received a visit by Heavenly Father and Jesus Christ that eventually led to instructions to reestablish the Church of Jesus Christ on the earth. Joseph did his best to teach the gospel, baptize converts, and establish a church. On April 6, 1830, the Church was officially organized in Fayette, New York. Of course, there were problems. Even the restored Church had to be staffed by human beings. In 1828, Joseph gave 116 pages of the Book of Mormon manuscript to Martin Harris—who immediately lost them. The Lord was not pleased (D&C 10:1–2).

In early 1837, the Kirtland Safety Society opened for business.[8] Joseph, perhaps not fully appreciating the conflict of interest in being a religious leader and a bank official, encouraged Saints to invest in the Safety Society.[9] On Joseph's assurances, Church members both invested and borrowed money, often to speculate in land. But it was very poor timing. Due to actions by the federal government, the "Panic of 1837" made a shambles of the national economy. Enemies of the Church worked to bring down the Safety Society. By June, faced with certain collapse, both Joseph and Sidney resigned from their positions in the business. All investors lost their money, including Joseph. The collapse plunged the Church into a financial crisis. Lawsuits and criminal charges followed. Once-faithful Church leaders apostatized and began working for the downfall of the Church. By January 1838, Joseph and Sidney had to leave Kirtland with their families to try to make a fresh start in Missouri.[10] The Church had lost much money and, worse, many faithful Saints. It was a blow from which it would take years to recover. Though his intentions were good in trying to provide his people with financial resources, Joseph had made a poor executive decision that had serious repercussions.

Polygamy

The prophet Jeremiah was commanded by the Lord to preach to the cities of Judah "all the words I command thee to speak unto them; diminish not a word." For his trouble, Jeremiah was taken and told, "Thou shalt surely die" (Jeremiah 26:1–8). This response to bad news is called "shooting the messenger" and is a common danger for prophets of God. Jeremiah survived that incident, but Abinadi (Mosiah 16:20), John the Baptist (Matthew 14:10), and others did not.

Of all of Joseph Smith's revelations, the one he is most remembered for in world history is that of polygamy. Polygamy is first mentioned in Genesis 4:19 and was practiced by the patriarchs Abraham, Isaac, and Jacob. As explained in the book of Jacob in the Book of Mormon, there are times when polygamy is needed, such as when the Lord needs to increase Church membership (Jacob 2:30). Since all of the Abrahamic covenants were being restored to the restored Church, polygamy was reintroduced as well. Joseph was commanded to institute polygamy into the Church.

If such a major doctrine was restored today, a three-inch-thick procedural manual from Church headquarters would accompany the announcement, but Joseph had no such manual. First, Joseph did not tell his wife Emma about his efforts to live the new law, an omission that was probably ill-advised. Joseph didn't even tell his brother Hyrum for a long time.[11] Consequently, rumors and gossip leaked out to the Church and the world regarding the practice and extent of polygamy. In hindsight, Joseph probably realized he could have better managed the introduction of such a difficult doctrine.

Last, Joseph did not have a succession plan in place. Upon his death, the leadership of the Church came into question. Some followed Joseph's son, Joseph Smith III, and started their own church. Sidney Rigdon also made a play for Church leadership, but Brigham Young eventually became the Church's president. The history of the Church and its survival could have been very different had the wrong leader been chosen at such a critical juncture.

COMPARED TO WHOM?

So we have established that Joseph Smith and other early Church leaders were human, with human frailties and mistaken perceptions. With 20/20 hindsight, we realize that they made some poor decisions. But if you are angry at Joseph Smith or other Church leaders in history because of the polygamy issue or some other reason, you must answer one question. If you consider Joseph Smith to be a poor prophet and leader of the Church of Jesus Christ, of all the people who have ever lived, who do you think *was* a great prophet and leader? Moses? Before Moses became the prophet, he was a murderer (Exodus 2:12). King David? As we know, David was an adulterer and the murderer of Uriah (2 Samuel 11). Peter? The Savior continually had to chastise Peter for mistakes. Peter tried to persuade Jesus to not go to Jerusalem for the Atonement, did not want Him to wash His feet, lopped off the ear of Malchus during the arrest, denied Christ three times, and then returned to fishing instead of taking over the presidency of the Church! The Savior Himself? Sorry, you're breaking rule #7. Your choice must be 100 percent human. Joseph Smith made mistakes as the prophet and leader of the Church, but they rather pale in comparison to mistakes made by other Church leaders over the history of the world. If you hold an individual to a standard *that has never been met by anyone else in the world*, one must look at your level of expectation. If your standard is a mythical person who doesn't make mistakes (or exist), then your critiques may merit a review.

If you are angry at a present-day Church leader, such as your bishop or stake president, to whom would you look as a replacement? Again, referring to rule #7, you must choose a human being. As noted, you are looking for someone who is responsible, humble, generous, and kind. They must have a good memory for names, have time to dedicate to the calling, and be willing to be awakened by calls in the middle of the night (and speak gently when answering the phone). Are you confident enough in your selection to be willing to take personal responsibility for your candidate's poor choices, offenses, and mistakes?

Finally, by the same measure, if you are angry with the Church for its actions, to what organization should we look as our standard? Do we look to a political party? A labor union? A law firm or large corporation? Each organization is staffed by fallible human beings, and I can guarantee that, with a simple investigation, we can find mistakes, abuses, and individual acts of selfishness, greed, and pride. To what standard do you wish to hold the Church? The organization you suggest must actually exist on earth.

If you can't find a person or organization that can be our gold standard, then maybe your anger should not be directed at the Church but rather at people in general. Church members are, after all, just a subset of the human population on earth. Each one of us has emotional weaknesses, pride, anxiety, insecurity, and anger issues. Church membership and weekly attendance at church are designed to make us better people, but it is a lifelong process to learn to control our natural tendencies. I look at my own emotions and reactions to others in social situations, when driving my car and at church, and I am continually disappointed in what I see. Usually, I am able to tamp down on those reactions before they are verbalized, but if you could ever witness my emotions from where I see them, you would probably be appalled. An old quote illustrates this reality: "The Church is a hospital for sinners, not a museum for Saints." At least as members of a church, we are trying to become better people.

Better Human Beings

Personally, I have always compared a church ward to a rock tumbler. Ward boundaries are established, and the members who live within those boundaries are all metaphorically placed into the rotating drum of the rock polisher. We see our fellow ward members each Sunday and during the week. Our children play together. We are given callings where we work together even more closely with others serving in the same church organization. We minister to one another. In the midst of all those repeated contacts, we become more polished and get better at social interaction. We develop empathy and learn to avoid rudeness. Our callings allow us to learn how to deal with toddlers, youth, adults, and the elderly.

But as one of those rocks, when a sharp corner is broken off, it hurts! Tempers flare, angry words are spoken, and feelings are hurt. We hope that we can learn to forgive, learn some wisdom from the painful experience, and move on, but sometimes a member will take offense, rebel at the whole polishing process, and choose to leave the rock tumbler. That is sad, because the polishing and self-improvement offered by church activity stops. Many members consider activity in their church to be a responsibility and a huge sink of time and resources. Ironically, members might better understand the need for church activity by looking at it from a purely selfish point of view. Being involved in church is intended to make you a better person. Truth be told, time spent in church is more educational than reading a self-improvement book at home. Fellowship at church is a shared experience. When done right, both parties should gain something from their interactions.

We sometimes call our ward our "ward family." That is a sweet sentiment . . . until I realize the hard work it takes just to hold my genealogical family together. A ward family means that I have yet *another* family to care for and fellowship? But considering my starting point is that of a flawed, prideful, self-absorbed human being, maybe I should welcome the additional learning opportunity.

Chapter 15

Our Perceptions of God

FOR THOSE WHO BELIEVE IN GOD but are angry with Him, I hope this book has helped you to see that your anger may be displaced. Mortal life has existed in many worlds over the course of millions of years. Our world is certainly not the first. It follows a proven pattern for teaching us wisdom and helping us choose righteousness. In this closing chapter, we need to address our perception of God. After all, those who are angry with God have a negative perception of who He is. Mistaken perceptions of God go all the way back to Cain. We all hope we have an accurate picture of God in our minds, but perceptions are fluid ideas and can change after we go through a traumatic experience, comfort loved ones, or just read a well-written book. Sometimes our perceptions are not fair to others, but it takes us awhile to recognize that fact.

It is interesting to note how our religious culture has changed over the years and how those trends have affected our perceptions of God today. Just as fads in fashion alter what we choose to wear, fads in religion affect how we choose to worship. One of those fads was called the New Age movement.

The New Age Movement

In the 1700s, philosophers, mystics, and scientists began investigations into the spiritual realm of angels, communication with the dead, and past lives. In the 1800s, pioneers of modern psychology added their teachings regarding the human will, the conscious and subconscious mind, dreams, and self-actualization. In the 1960s, part of this movement looked to psychedelic drugs to help reach a higher state of consciousness. In the 1970s, holistic medicine became a trend, bringing with it many of the practices of the Far East, such as meditation, yoga, acupuncture, shiatsu, and natural therapies. Beliefs were borrowed from Hinduism, Taoism, and Buddhism. These elements were all combined to form what has become known as the New Age movement.

Also beginning in the rebellious years of the 1960s, a general discontent with established religions made itself known. Church services were considered to be scripted, parochial, and boring. Religions were accused of being overly judgmental, with outdated expectations of their membership. Many people wanted a spiritual awakening yet a separation from mainstream religion. The New Age blend of Far East traditions, gurus, mysticism, and personal spiritual connection offered an exciting answer to those desires. The philosophy rejected religious doctrine and dogma and encouraged followers to choose their own individual approach to spiritual practice.

Some of the practices of the New Age movement—massage, yoga, meditation, and a holistic approach to health—survive today and are generally recognized for their benefits. Many of the fringe elements of the movement—crystal power, channeling of spirits, shamanism, etc.—were left behind. The New Age movement continued to evolve, much of it blending with "New Thought" teachings that had begun in the early 1900s. Then the movement took an interesting turn from seeking spiritual health to seeking personal wealth. As explained in one book on the New Age,

> It was based on personal motivation—on the idea, central to the American dream, that we all have the potential to achieve wealth, success and happiness if we have the drive and vision to bring it about . . . Introducing the elements of "self-help" and "success" to the holistic concept of inner balance and wellbeing was decisive in the birthing of what has now become known as the New Age movement.[1]

Besides the goal of a celestial reward, followers of the New Age/New Thought theology wanted wealth and success in this life. While spiritual blessings were fine, new agers also wanted successful careers and summer homes. But the God of the Bible, especially the New Testament, preached humility, sacrifice, service, and a focus on spiritual things. To fit the demands of New Age thinkers, a redefinition of God had to take place. Certain New Age teachers even changed God's name. This led to teachings like the following:

> When you focus your thoughts on something you want, and you hold that focus, you are in that moment summoning what you want with the mightiest power in the Universe. . . . What if your feelings are actually communication from the *Universe* to let you know what you are thinking?[2]

> I teach that we should stop thinking—that we should still the mind—and when that happens we are awakened to a Higher Source, the Eternal, the I Am, or whatever you care to call it. I train people through a process called 'centering' to make contact, to be open, to wake up to this Higher Source.[3]

Blending religion with gaining materialistic blessings has continued, gradually becoming what is now called the "Prosperity Gospel," from which we receive the following teachings:

> Get beyond the barriers of your past and start expecting God to do great things in your life . . . God may intervene in your situation, replacing your supervisor so you can be promoted. One day, you may run that entire company![4]

It is probably liberating to rename God and then imagine Him to be whatever you want Him to be. I am sure most people would choose to imagine a very giving and forgiving God, one who will be generous in this life and lenient in the next. Sending thoughts out into the universe and expecting God to do great things in your life sounds easier than petitioning Him for blessings. The problem with imagining the kind of God you want to worship is that you are just imagining it. The universe is a large vacuum-filled space with intermittent galaxies. No one can explain how the universe can provide blessings, no matter how hard you try to project them. Calling God a Higher Source or Prime Mover does not change the rules of how we should address Him nor how He will respond.

The most accurate image of our Christian god is the one that we build from the scriptures. Many people don't want that perception anymore. In a recent Pew study, when asked if they believed in God, 18 percent of Christian-affiliated respondents indicated that they believed in a God, but not the God of the Bible. Of Jewish-affiliated respondents, 56 percent replied that they believed in God, but not the God of the Old Testament.

Sadly but not surprisingly, younger Americans are the least likely to believe in the biblical God. Only 43 percent of young adults between the ages of eighteen and twenty-nine believe in the God of the Bible. Fully 39 percent of this age group believes in a higher power or spiritual force that is not the God described in the scriptures.[5]

The problem with not having a scriptural perception of God, as these New Age teachings have encouraged, is that you have nothing upon which to base your religion or your prayers. As one Christian author explained,

> God wants us to use our faith and pray. But we can focus so much on the importance of our faith and our prayers that we forget about God and think it is our faith and prayers that perform the miracle, rather than the God to whom we pray and in whom we have faith as we pray. If we fall into that trap, we become convinced that if our prayers are not being answered, it's because we aren't praying hard enough or long enough, or because our faith is simply weak.[6]

Our Perceptions of the Savior

I have seen many different images of the Savior in my life. Several artists try to emphasize the love and humility of the Savior. They gave Him a diminutive stature, soulful eyes, and a weak beard. He looks very meek, merciful, and soft-spoken, but I believe these artists have gone too far. By emphasizing the humility and meekness of the Savior, they have made Him look weak. With this image of Jesus Christ in my mind, I won't worry too much about my behavior on earth. Whatever sins I have committed, the Savior depicted in these images will assuredly forgive me whether I repent or not. Even worse, many images of Jesus Christ are associated with Christmas, so He is portrayed as a baby. That too is a very comforting image. What could be less intimidating than an infant baby boy? With a baby as our judge, we can be comforted in the expectation that we can do whatever we want in this life and the judgment will still be easy.

So let's go to the other extreme. I would like you to consider one more image of the Savior. Call to your mind the painting by Arnold Friberg of Captain Moroni standing in front of the Standard of Liberty flag—and consider this as an image of the Savior in His role as bringer of justice. Moroni is, of course, a military man, large in stature with a muscular build. His face is strong. He has a full beard and eyes that will not tolerate nonsense. He wears armor and grasps a large, two-edged sword in his right hand. I realize that the artist was not trying to depict Jesus Christ in this painting, but images are flexible. With this Moroni-like image of the Savior in your mind, notice how your attitude toward God shifts. My dedication to obedience certainly increases. I am not going to be as nonchalant about my faithfulness, because this depiction of the Savior will certainly hold me accountable. Personally, I admit that I prefer this image. If this is what the Savior looks like, the first time I see Him, I know I will drop to my knees—not because I am told to do so, but because it will be the most natural thing to do in the presence of my God and King.

The goal of this book has been to change your perceptions, because perceptions are important. We should hope for accuracy in our mental images, because they will have a significant effect on how we live our lives and regard the gospel.

Our Perception of God the Father

Our perceptions often change with our emotions. If you have thought of God as a kindly and benevolent grandfather, maybe you should also recognize that He is the Creator and Ruler of this world. If you have thought of God the Father as an all-powerful overlord who permits evil to cause suffering to you and the rest of the world, I hope you can now recognize the requirements of earth life that God must maintain. God loves you, and He is on your side. He listens to your prayers, and He answers those prayers the best He can, given the rules that limit Him.

To summarize the perception that I hope you have of our earth and our Heavenly Father, God is a kind Father who had to ask you to leave your home in the premortal existence because you were bored and aimless. It was time for you to go to earth to continue your eternal progression. The plan was explained to you and, if you are reading this book, you agreed to it.

With God the Father supervising and the Savior and others doing the legwork, the earth was built to help you gather knowledge and learn wisdom. Your body was designed to teach you to care for it or cause you painful consequences when you don't. The earth included elements that allowed life to be possible—gravity, water, wind, magma, etc.—but could kill you if you did not afford them the proper respect.

The earth was designed to be a place of faith, and strict rules were put into place to keep it that way. God has had to follow these non-interference rules for millennia, since it was decreed that men and women could only learn about Him through a spiritual search, not a statistical study.

One of the rules of earth was that you must do work to make your way in this world. You must learn to labor, provide for your family, and organize your home such that entropy and disorder do not rule.

We don't know the reasons for where, when, and into what family we are born, but we do have to play the hand we are dealt. Whatever our circumstances, we can learn wisdom in this life and, we hope, choose righteousness as we do so.

We must accept that life on earth is meant to be temporary. Aging and death are as much a part of life as birth and childhood.

We must suffer the consequences of others' bad decisions, whether they are family, friends, or world leaders. The first step of learning forgiveness is to be harmed or offended by someone. God provided us a world where we can practice requesting and offering forgiveness on a regular basis.

Finally, there is an obvious rule that the Church of Jesus Christ must be staffed with people. Fallible human beings must run church leadership, church administration, welfare programs, youth programs, and the like. Due to this fact, we can expect disputes and arguments among them. Still, I marvel at the criticism I hear of good people or past leaders of the Church who were just trying to do their best at their voluntary jobs and callings.

EPILOGUE

IT IS EXCITING TO LIVE IN A PHASE of our eternal life that holds so much challenge and danger. Here we have a chance to prove ourselves worthy of being trusted with power and authority in our next life.

Earth life may be harder and harsher than you think it should be. Your prayers may not be answered as quickly and precisely as you hope. The consequences of your own mistakes and those of loved ones may seem impossible to bear at times, but knowing there are rules in effect for this mortal probation can actually be comforting.

Presently we "see through a glass darkly," so though we can recognize a few of the rules of earth, we don't understand them all yet. When we finally have the full story, from our premortal existence to our afterlife and Judgment, we will understand everything about this life and the reasons for its laws. For now, know that Heavenly Father and His Son are watching over us, both making sure we are following the rules and helping us whenever they can.

Notes

Chapter 1—Is God to Blame for Tragedy?

1. "Hurricane Katrina, August 23–31, 2005," Service Assessment, National Weather Service (NWS), Silver Spring, MD; see nws.noaa.gov/om/assessments/pdfs/Katrina.pdf; accessed on March 5, 2020.
2. Gordon B. Hinckley, "If Ye Are Prepared Ye Shall Not Fear," *Ensign*, Nov. 2005.
3. Harold S. Kushner, *When Bad Things Happen to Good People* (New York: Anchor Books, 1981).
4. Brent L. Top, *Why Bad Things Happen to Good People* (Salt Lake City: Bookcraft, 1991).
5. Elisabeth Kubler-Ross and David Kessler, *On Grief and Grieving* (New York: Scribner, 2005), 7, 13, 17.
6. Ross and Kessler, *On Grief and Grieving.*
7. "Three Startling Facts about California's Camp Fire," *USA Today*; see usatoday.com/story/news/2018/11/20/camp-fire-3-startling-facts/2064758002; accessed March 5, 2020.
8. Joseph Smith, *Teachings of the Prophet Joseph Smith* (Salt Lake City: Deseret Book, 1997), 162–63.
9. Michael Austin, *Re-reading Job* (Draper, UT: Greg Kofford Books, 2014), 5.
10. Austin, *Re-reading Job,* 6.
11. Marvin J. Ashton, "If Thou Endure It Well," *Ensign*, Nov. 1984.
12. Allister E. McGrath, *Historical Theology*, 2 ed. (Chichester, West Sussex, UK: Wiley-Blackwell, 2013), 185–87. See elearning.thirdmill.org/theme/standard_thirdmill/lessons/BBT1text.html; accessed March 5, 2020.
13. George Q. Cannon, *Gospel Truth* (Salt Lake City: Deseret Book, 1987), 301–2.

14. Jeffrey R. Holland, *On Earth as It Is in Heaven* (Salt Lake City, UT: Deseret Book, 1989), 162.

15. Kushner, *When Bad Things Happen to Good People.*

CHAPTER 2—LEARNING WISDOM VERSUS CHOOSING RIGHTEOUSNESS

1. "Safety on the Road," National Safety Council, nsc.org/road-safety; accessed March 6, 2019.
2. Robert Fulghum, *All I Really Need to Know I learned in Kindergarten* (New York City: Ivy Books, 1988), 4.
3. Paul Ekman, *Emotion in the Human Face* (Los Altos, CA: Malor Books, 2013).
4. James E. Talmage, *Jesus the Christ* (Salt Lake City: Deseret Book, 1974), 329.
5. Spencer W. Kimball, *Faith Precedes a Miracle* (Salt Lake City: Deseret Book, 1972), 98.
6. C. S. Lewis, *Mere Christianity* (New York: Harper Collins, 1952), 204–5.
7. David O. McKay, "Man's Free Agency—An Eternal Principle of Progress," *Improvement Era,* Dec. 1965.
8. Kimball, *Faith Precedes a Miracle*, 96.

CHAPTER 3—THE PREMORTAL EXISTENCE

1. Joseph Smith, *History of the Church* (Salt Lake City: Deseret Book, 1978), 6:312; italics added. From a discourse given by Joseph Smith on April 7, 1844, in Nauvoo, Illinois; reported by Wilford Woodruff, Willard Richards, Thomas Bullock, and William Clayton.
2. Smith, *History*, 6:308.
3. John L. Lund, *Encyclopedia of Mormonism*, ed. Daniel H. Ludlow (New York: Macmillan, 1992), 328–29.
4. "The Family: A Proclamation to the World," *Ensign* or *Liahona,* Nov. 2010, 129.
5. Smith, *History of the Church*, 6:314.
6. Neil A. Maxwell, *We Will Prove Them Herewith* (Salt Lake City: Deseret Book, 1982), 3.
7. Thomas S. Monson, "Invitation to Exaltation," *Ensign*, June 1993, 4.

CHAPTER 4—RULE 1: THE EARTH MUST BE A PLACE OF FAITH

1. See "statistics" at merriam-webster.com/dictionary/statistics.
2. Erik Gregersen, *The Britannica Guide to Statistics and Probability* (New York: Britannica Educational Publishing, 2011).
3. Charles Wheelan, *Naked Statistics* (New York: W.W. Norton, 2013).
4. H. Benson, J. Dusek, and J. B. Sherwood, "Study of the therapeutic effects of intercessory prayer (STEP) in cardiac bypass patients: a multicenter randomized trial of uncertainty and certainty of receiving intercessory prayer," *American Heart Journal* (2006) 151, 934–42.
5. Benedict Carey, "Long-Awaited Medical Study Questions the Power of Prayer," *New York Times*, Mar. 31, 2006.

CHAPTER 5—RULE 2: YOU MUST DO WORK

1. Donald McQuarrie and Peter Rock, *General Chemistry* (New York: W. H. Freeman, 1987).

CHAPTER 6—RULE 3: THE EARTH IS A DANGEROUS PLACE

1. YouTube, "Neil deGrasse Tyson on God," April 30, 2017. See youtube.com/watch?v=I0nXG02tpDw; accessed March 9, 2020.
2. *National Vital Statistics Reports*, Table 18, Vol. 65, No. 4, June 30, 2016.
3. *National Vital Statistics*, ibid.
4. *National Vital Statistics*, ibid.
5. John P. Rafferty, *Climate and Climate Change* (New York: Britannica Educational Publishing, 2011), 15.
6. William Bryant Logan, *Air* (New York: W.W. Norton, 2012), 29–30.
7. Rafferty, *Climate and Climate Change*, 39.
8. Robert Decker and Barbara Decker, *Volcanoes* (New York: W. H. Freeman, 1998), 15.
9. Decker and Decker, *Volcanoes*, ibid.

10. Claire Suddath, "Mt. Vesuvius," *Time* Magazine, Aug. 31, 2010. See content.time.com/time/specials/packages/article/0,28804,2014572_2014574_2014626,00.html; accessed March 9, 2020.

11. Lisa Wald, "Earthquake Hazards," USGS, nd. See earthquake.usgs.gov/learn/facts.php; accessed March 9, 2020.

12. The Economist, "A remarkable account of the 2011 tsunami in Japan," August 10, 2007. See economist.com/books-and-arts/2017/08/19/a-remarkable-account-of-the-2011-tsunami-in-japan; accessed March 9, 2020.

13. Rabbi Harold S. Kushner, *When Bad Things Happen to Good People* (New York: Anchor Books, 1981), 68.

CHAPTER 7—LEARNING AS A WORLD

1. Frederick R. Cartwright, *Disease and History* (New York: Barnes & Noble, 1972), 7.
2. Jennifer Wright, *Get Well Soon* (New York: Harry Holt, 2017), 13.
3. Cartwright, *Disease and History*, 8.
4. Cartwright, *Disease and History*, 15.
5. Wright, *Get Well Soon*, 29, 40.
6. Lynette Lezzoni, *Influenza 1918* (New York: TV Books, 1999).
7. Cartwright, *Disease and History*, 37.
8. Sean Martin, *The Black Death* (Edison, NJ: Chartwell Books, 2007), 50.
9. Jared Diamond, *Guns, Germs & Steel* (New York: W.W. Norton, 1997), 201.
10. Wright, *Get Well Soon*, 77.
11. Diamond, *Guns, Germs & Steel*, 202.
12. Wright, *Get Well Soon*, 68.
13. Alfred Jay Bollet, *Plagues and Poxes* (New York: Demos Medical Publishing, 2004), 106.
14. Lynette Izzoni, *Influenza 1918* (New York: TV Books, 1999), 66–67.
15. Bollet, *Plagues and Poxes*, 103.
16. Centers for Disease Control and Prevention, "2014–2016 Ebola Outbreak in West Africa," cdc.gov/vhf/ebola/history/2014-2016-outbreak/index.html; accessed March 10, 2020.

17. Centers for Disease Control and Prevention, "Prevalence of Autism Spectrum Disorder Among Children Aged 8 Years—Autism and Developmental Disabilities Monitoring Network, 11 Sites, United States, 2014," cdc.gov/mmwr/volumes/67/ss/ss6706a1.htm (April 27, 2018 / 67 [6]), 1–23; accessed March 10, 2020.
18. CDC, "Prevalence of Autism Spectrum Disorder," ibid.
19. Peggy J. Parks, *Autism* (San Diego, CA: ReferencePoint, 2009), 32.
20. Centers for Disease Control and Prevention, "Treatment for Autism Spectrum Disorder" (August 2019), cdc.gov/ncbddd/autism/treatment.html; accessed March 10, 2020.
21. Mental Health America, "ADHD and ADD," mentalhealthamerica.net/conditions/adhd-and-kids; accessed March 10, 2020.
22. Melissa L. Danielson, Rebecca H. Bitsko, Reem M. Ghandour, Joseph R. Holbrook, Michael D. Kogan, and Stephen J. Blumberg, "Prevalence of Parent-Reported ADHD Diagnosis and Associated Treatment among U.S. Children and Adolescents, 2016," *Journal of Clinical Child & Adolescent Psychology*; Volume 47, Issue 2 (2018).
23. Mental Health American, "ADHD and ADD," mentalhealthamerica.net/conditions/adhd-and-kids; accessed March 10, 2020.

Chapter 8—Rule 4: You Must Play the Hand You Are Dealt

1. Spencer W. Kimball, "Marriage and Divorce," speeches.byu.edu/talks/spencer-w-kimball_marriage-divorce/, devotional address given at Brigham Young University on September 7, 1976; accessed on March 10, 2020.
2. Steven J. Heine, *DNA Is Not Destiny* (New York: W.W. Norton, 2017), 15.
3. Frances S. Collins, *The Language of God* (New York: Free Press, 2006), 131.
4. Steph Yin, "Cold Tolerance among Inuit May Come from Extinct Human Relatives," *New York Times* (December 23, 2016), nytimes.com/2016/12/23/science/inuit-greenland-denisovans.html; accessed on March 10, 2020.
5. *Professional Guide to Diseases*, 8th ed. (Ambler, PA: Lippincott Williams & Wilkins), 1.

6. *Professional Guide*, 6.
7. Luca Passamonti, "What your Brain Structure Says about your Personality," *The Conversation*, Jan. 25, 2017, theconversation.com/what-your-brain-structure-says-about-your-personality-71826; accessed March 10, 2020.
8. David S. Moore, *The Developing Genome* (New York: Oxford University Press, 2015), 22, 213–14.

Chapter 9—Rule 5: Temporal Life Must Be Temporary

1. Rick Baudé, *Almost Everything You Need to Know about Termites and Wood Destroying Organisms* (self-published, 2007).
2. Bruce G. Marcot, "A Review of the Role of Fungi in Wood Decay of Forest Ecosystems," U.S. Department of Agriculture Pacific Northwest Research Station, Aug. 2017.
3. Laura Zuckerman, "Cost of fighting U.S. wildfires topped $2 billion in 2017," Reuters, reuters.com/article/us-usa-wildfires/cost-of-fighting-u-s-wildfires-topped-2-billion-in-2017-idUSKCN1BQ01F; accessed March 11, 2020.
4. Cory Nealon, "Total Cost of Fire in the United States," Fire Protection Research Foundation, Department of Industrial and Systems Engineering, University at Buffalo (NY), Dec. 1, 2017.
5. Stephen J. Gould, *The Book of Life* (New York: W.W. Norton, 1993), 132, 154.
6. Larry Copeland, "Life expectancy in the USA hits a record high," *USA Today*, Oct. 8, 2014, usatoday.com/story/news/nation/2014/10/08/us-life-expectancy-hits-record-high/16874039/; accessed March 11, 2020.
7. Bill Gifford, *Spring Chicken* (New York: Grand Central Publishing, 2015), 18.
8. Christine Overall, *Aging, Death, and Human Longevity* (Los Angeles: Univ. of California Press, 2003),
9. Xiao Dong, Brandon Milholland, and Jan Vijg, "Evidence for a limit to human life span," *Nature*, Vol. 538 (2016), 257–58.
10. Cameron Diaz and Sandra Bark, *Longevity Book* (New York: Harper Collins, 2016), 83.
11. WebMD.com, "Stop Making These Common Beauty Mistakes," webmd.com/beauty; accessed March 11, 2020.

12. Diaz and Bark, *Longevity Book*, 83.
13. Gifford, *Spring Chicken*, 18.
14. Diaz and Bark, *Longevity Book*, 87–88.
15. Atul Gawande, *Being Mortal* (New York: Picador, 2014), 27–28.
16. Gawande, *Being Mortal*, 31.
17. Sherwin Nuland, *How We Die: Reflections on Life's Final Chapter* (New York: Kropf, 1994), 87.

Chapter 10—Rule 6: We Must Suffer the Consequences of Others' Bad Decisions

1. Robert Weldon Whalen, "War Losses (Germany)," International Encyclopedia of the First World War (WWI), encyclopedia.1914-1918-online.net/article/war_losses_germany; accessed March 11, 2020.
2. Terry Burrows, *Visual History of the Twentieth Century* (London: Carlton Books, 1999), 90.
3. Burrows, *Visual History*, 173.
4. "World War 2 Statistics," Second World War History (2003–2020), second-worldwarhistory.com/world-war-2-statistics.asp; accessed March 11, 2020.
5. Burrows, *Visual History*, 68–69.
6. Martin Gilbert, *A History of the Twentieth Century* (New York: William Morrow, 1997), 464.
7. Burrows, *Visual History*, 68–69.
8. Burrows, *Visual History*, 95.
9. Burrows, *Visual History*, 116.
10. Gilbert, *A History*, 734.

Chapter 11—Everyone Must Obey the Rules of Earth

1. James E. Talmage, *Jesus the Christ* (Salt Lake City: Deseret Book, 1974), 58.
2. Talmage, *Jesus the Christ*, 69.
3. "Spartacus," *New World Encyclopedia*, newworldencyclopedia.org/entry/Spartacus; accessed March 11, 2020.

4. Pierre Barbet, *Doctor at Calvary*, reprint ed. (Washington, DC: Allegro Editions, 2014), 47.

5. Barbet, *Doctor at Calvary*, 49.

CHAPTER 12: PRAYER—ASKING FOR EXCEPTIONS TO THE RULES

1. Howard W. Hunter, *Teachings of Howard W. Hunter* (Salt Lake City: Deseret Book, 1997), 39.

2. See "Miracle," merriam-webster.com/dictionary/miracle.

3. Center for Disease Control and Prevention, "Achievements in Public Health, 1900-1999: Healthier Mothers and Babies," Oct. 1, 1999, cdc.gov/mmwr/preview/mmwrhtml/mm4838a2.htm; accessed March 12, 2020.

4. Center for Disease Control and Prevention, "Arthritis," cdc.gov/arthritis/; accessed March 12, 2020.

5. Pew Research Center, "U.S. Public Becoming Less Religious," Nov. 3, 2015, pewforum.org/2015/11/03/u-s-public-becoming-less-religious/; accessed March 12, 2020.

6. The UN Refugee Agency, "Figures at a Glance," 2001–2020, unhcr.org/en-us/figures-at-a-glance.html; accessed March 12, 2020.

CHAPTER 13—THE PROBLEM WITH MIRACLES

1. T. C. Christensen and Jolene S. Allphin, *More Than Miracles* (Salt Lake City, Deseret Book, 2012), 8.

2. Eric Metaxas, *Miracles: What They Are, Why They Happen, and How They Can Change Your Life* (New York: Dutton, 2014), 5, 15.

3. "Miracle," Merriam-Webster.com, merriam-webster.com/dictionary/miracle; accessed March 12, 2020.

4. Gabrielle Berstein, *May Cause Miracles* (New York: Harmony Books, 2013), 6.

Chapter 14—Rule 7: The Church of Jesus Christ Must Be Staffed with Humans

1. Jeffrey R. Holland, "Lord, I Believe," *Ensign*, May 2013, 94.
2. Bart D. Ehrman, *Forged* (New York: HarperOne, 2011).
3. Ehrman, *Forged.*
4. Jean-Pierre Isbouts, *Archaeology of the Bible* (Washington, DC: National Geographic, 2016), 299–301.
5. Edward A. Ryan, "Spanish Inquisition," Britannica Encyclopedia, 2015–2019, britannica.com/topic/Spanish-Inquisition; accessed March 12, 2020.
6. Barrie Ruth Strauss, *The Catholic Church—A Concise History* (New York: Hippocrene Books, 1992), 142–43.
7. Karen Armstrong, *Fields of Blood* (New York: Alfred A. Knopf, 2014), 246.
8. Richard Lyman Bushman, *Joseph Smith Rough Stone Rolling* (New York: Vintage Books, 2005), 330.
9. *Saints* (Salt Lake City: The Church of Jesus Christ of Latter-day Saints, 2018), 261.
10. *Saints*, 299, 304.
11. *Saints,* 491.

Chapter 15—Our Perceptions of God

1. Nevill Drury, *The New Age* (London: Thomas & Hudson, 2004), 121.
2. Rhonda Byrne, *The Secret* (New York: Atria Books, 2006), 14, 33.
3. Alexander Everett, founder of Mind Dynamics and Inward Bound, as quoted in *The New Age* by Nevill Drury (London: Thames and Hudson, 2004), 125.
4. Joel Osteen, *Your Best Life Now* (New York: Warner Faith, 2004), 9, 22.
5. Pew Research Center, "When Americans Say They Believe in God, What Do They Mean?" April 25, 2018, pewforum.org/2018/04/25/when-americans-say-they-believe-in-god-what-do-they-mean/, 11, 16; accessed March 12, 2020.
6. Eric Metaxas, *Miracles: What They Are, Why They Happen, and How They Can Change Your Life* (New York: Dutton, 2014), 71.

About the Author

SCOTT R. FRAZER, PhD (chemistry, University of Arizona), joined The Church of Jesus Christ of Latter-day Saints when he was nineteen years old and left on a Church mission to Mexico City a year later. Upon his return to Colorado, Scott completed his bachelor's degree, married his wife, Cheri, and then completed his doctorate in analytical chemistry. His work history includes research roles in a variety of industries.

Since joining the Church, Scott has pursued a study of the overlaps between science, history, and religious doctrine. One can learn much about our spiritual lives from the study of its interactions with the material universe and earth's history. Scott's writings are dedicated to shed a different light on the gospel by observing the world around us.

Having lived in numerous locations across the U.S., Scott and Cheri now reside in Saratoga Springs, Utah, to be near their four children and their families.